Streets of
San Francisco

D0723380

STOCKTON Street Tunnel

Streets of San Francisco

The Origins of Street and Place Names

Louis K. Loewenstein

Illustrated by **Penny deMoss**

 WILDERNESS PRESS · Berkeley

THIRD EDITION April 1996
Second printing February 2002
Third printing November 2002

Drawings by Penny deMoss
Book Design by Anne Iverson
Cover Design by Larry B. Van Dyke
Cover Photo © 1996 Lombard Street by Ken Glaser, Jr.

Library of Congress Card Catalog Number 96-3537
International Standard Book Number 0-89997-192-X

Manufactured in the United States of America

Published by **Wilderness Press**
      1200 5th Street
      Berkeley, CA 94710

      www.wildernesspress.com
      Toll free (800) 443-7227
      FAX (510) 558-1696

      Contact us for a free catalog.

Library of Congress Cataloging-in-Publication Data
Loewenstein, Louis K.
      Streets of San Francisco : the origins of street and place names / Louis K. Loewenstein; illus-
trated by Penny deMoss.—3rd ed.
            p.   cm.
      Includes bibliographical references.
      ISBN 0-89997-192-X
      1. San Francisco (Calif.)—History. 2. Street Names—California—San Francisco. 3. Names,
Geographical—California—San Francisco.
      I. Title.
F869.S375A2 1996
917.94'61'0014-dc20   96-3537
                                             CIP

Dedication

to Neyde

ACKNOWLEDGMENTS

While I am completely responsible for this book's contents, I would like to thank the following, whose suggestions and insights only and immeasurably improved it.

Hamilton Barrett; Louis Bernstein; Bob Berlo; Michael Blanchard; Don Burkholder, San Francisco Redevelopment Agency; Josephine Cole; Randolph Delehanty; Robert M. De Wolfe; Carolyn Elderberry; Sarah Elias; Peter Garland; Corbet Hanchett; Gladys Hansen, City Archivist and curator of the San Francisco Public Library's History Room; George Holly, Gray Line Sight Seeing Tours; Beverly Hoppe; Anne Iverson; Patricia Keats; Karl Kortum, Director of the San Francisco Maritime Museum; Michael Lampen, Archivist, Grace Episcopal Cathedral; Sandra Larson, Librarian of the Presidio Army Museum; Eugene Mattingly, St. Francis Square; James McCarthy, former Planning Director, City of San Francisco; John B. McGloin, University of San Francisco; Wandaline Perelli, an extraordinary copy editor; Frances Roberts, Real Estate Department, Presidio of San Francisco; Edward Roper; Eric Saul, Curator of the Presidio Army Museum; Father Tom Seagrave, Associate Pastor, St. Peter's Catholic Church; Linda Seekamp, Archivist, St. Mary's; Brian Shea; Dr. Charles Albert Shumate, former President of the California Historical Society; Louise Teather; Neyde Trindade; Warren White, City College of San Francisco; Mary Elizabeth Williams; and Wes Willoughby, San Francisco Redevelopment Agency.

I made extensive use of the following libraries, to which I also owe a debt of gratitude: The Bancroft Library of the University of California, the California Historical Society Library, the San Francisco Public Library History Room, and the Sons of California Pioneers Library.

Contents

PACIFIC Avenue at Presidio Wall

INTRODUCTION

In an article about San Francisco streets, the *San Jose Pioneer* of September 15, 1897, noted: "But outside of a few prominent streets . . . and those bearing the names of presidents little seems to be known among San Franciscans as to whom and what the pioneers were whose names remain on the maps of their city."

What was true almost a century ago is equally true today. Of course, some books, articles, and newspaper stories on the origins of San Francisco street names have appeared in the past ten decades. But no general work—until this one—has dealt comprehensively with the topic.

For a variety of confounding reasons, any work such as this must be somewhat tentative and incomplete; there are undoubtedly mistakes of both omission and commission in the following pages. For example, despite my best efforts, I was able to discover the origins of the names of only approximately 1,300 of San Francisco's 1,735 non-numbered and non-lettered streets. Where I am not positive about the derivation of the name, I have used the words "probably" or "possibly." In some other instances, however, even where this *caveat* is missing, there may still be errors. Naturally, I would like to be made aware of these misstatements so that an improved edition might appear some day. So I encourage you to submit corrections and additional information to Wilderness Press, the publisher of this book.

The fact that I was not able to unearth all of the origins of the street names merits an explanation. In the first place, the great fire following the 1906 earthquake destroyed many city records (along with the city's new City Hall). For example, 28 alleys and courts and more than three dozen streets were given new names in 1882. Yet no records explaining who or what these streets were named for exist (see Appendix). The most prolific spate of street naming occurred in 1909, when the Street Names Committee of the Board of Supervisors gave almost 100 streets new names. But for the most part this committee's deliberations appear to be lost to history. Indeed, the documentation of street names in general is less than one would hope for. Street name changes are approved by the Board of Supervisors after review and approval by the Department of Public Works. But the rationale for these changes does not usually appear in the *Proceedings of the Board of Supervisors* or in the ordinances of the *Municipal Records*. Only the name change itself is found. Thus, the researcher is often left to intuition, judgment, and even wits in the search for the origins of street names.

Several guidelines used in the preparation of this book should be mentioned. First, very little anecdotal material is given about well-known figures such as Christopher Columbus. Considerably more biographical data is offered for such local luminaries as James Lick and James Fair. Second, I have tried to find the origin of geographical names, such as Nottingham Place, even though these words are usually taken for granted.

Finally, I have excluded the names of several street groupings whose origins are obvious. These include streets which were named by the Redevelopment Agency for precious and semi-precious gems in the 1960s, and those of thoroughfares named for trees.

Though San Francisco's streets are constantly being named and re-named, one can distinguish four periods during which the activity was at its height. The first of these is associated with four early surveys of the city which took place in the decade after 1839, when San Francisco was in its infancy.

Before the Gold Rush, the naming of the City's streets accompanied the efforts of the municipal surveyors to lay out and map the lots and blocks in the village of Yerba Buena (which became San Francisco on January 30, 1847). In the Spring of 1839, Governor Juan Alvarado directed Yerba Buena's Mayor Don Francisco Guerrero to have a survey made of the muddy, little community. In the fall of that year, Guerrero chose Jean Jacques Vioget, a Swiss sailor, tavernkeeper, and surveyor, to map the area bounded by what are now Pacific, Montgomery, Sacramento, and Grant. To Grant Avenue goes the honor of being San Francisco's oldest street. It was laid out in the late 1830s by William Richardson, the village's first inhabitant, and was called Calle de Fundación, or Foundation Street—an appropriate name for the first street of what was to become one of the world's great cities. Incidentally, Richardson's home, called a "rough shanty of boards" by Richard Henry Dana, was in what is now the 800 block of Grant between Washington and Clay.

In 1846, Lt. Washington A. Bartlett, Yerba Buena's military Mayor, commissioned Jasper O'Farrell to resurvey and extend the town. O'Farrell, an Irish engineer who had lived in Philadelphia and Valparaiso, Chile, before coming to California, based his plan on that of Philadelphia, considered at the time an excellent example of urban planning. (It should be mentioned that seven years earlier in *contra* distinction, Vioget had been influenced by New York City.) As a consequence some of the street names in these early surveys, such as Broadway and Greenwich, were inspired by New York while others, such as Lombard, Sansome, Chestnut, Filbert, Pine, and Market, are borrowed from Philadelphia.

During the Gold Rush, the town exploded in size and O'Farrell fever-ishly continued his surveying by extending the street lines in all directions (including straight into the Bay, thus creating underwater "paper blocks"). O'Farrell also laid out a second gridiron south of the original one which was tilted 45 degrees from the first plan. Between the two grids, O'Farrell planned Market Street to run from the Bay toward Mission Dolores. The surveys were totally insensitive to the contour of the town's hills and the undulations of its shoreline. They superimposed a dull grid plan—perhaps appropriate for Philadelphia's level ground—onto the wonderfully varied texture of San Francisco's landscape. Thus regularity and consistency dominated and froze into place what could have been an exciting and handsome array of streets that respected and enhanced the natural envi-ronment. Nowhere is this lack of imagination more evident than in the creation of two separate grids on the two sides of Market Street. Instead of uniting the City, Market separates it into two distinct areas by creating a traffic pattern that is inconsistent, irregular, and frustrating.

O'Farrell's design was further extended by City Surveyor William M. Eddy in 1849. The urban historian Rodger Lotchin has written, "Given the fact that William Eddy . . . stayed drunk a goodly portion of his working day, it is a wonder that the [plan] turned out as well as it did." The fourth surveyor in this early period was J. J. Hoff, about whom very little is known. In those days streets tended to be named for pioneers and their friends or relatives, for prominent civic officials or their friends, for the ships which brought settlers to California's golden shores, or for home towns and districts in the East, in England, or on the Continent.

The second street naming phase took place around the Civil War. Patriotic names or names associated with American history became popular. For instance, streets in Noe Valley are named for Civil War battles at Chattanooga and Vicksburg. Real-estate developers also began thematic projects. The University Homestead Association, for example, chose the names of prestigious eastern colleges and universities for their streets. A group of streets were named for European capital cities and countries in the 1860s by the Excelsior Homestead Association in what is known today as the Excelsior neighborhood. During this era, as the City expanded in all directions (including into the Bay, where those underwater "paper lots" became landfill), the city fathers used numbered streets and avenues; by 1876, two sets of numbered streets as well as one set of numbered avenues had emerged. This extended Eddy's original numbering system, which had been limited to only five streets.

The third street naming epoch was begun by the 1909 Committee on Street Names. Its charge was to bring a sense of order to what had by then become a chaotic process. The Committee's report acknowledged that "among the conspicuous mistakes are the use of the alphabet and the overworking of the numerals . . . the use of the letters of the alphabet is a cheap and indefensible expedient resorted to only when imagination is lacking." The conscientious street namers observed, "Other California cities of Spanish origin have availed themselves of the musical names associated with its discoverers and founders and made the most of our common inheritance [but] we have made very little of it." So they advocated giving the numbered avenues names that would commemorate saints and men prominent in the days of Spanish rule. The supervisors representing the affected districts objected to the proposal on the grounds that "Spain was one of the most cruel and bloodthirsty nations in Europe . . . and because of . . . the difficulty the conductors on street cars would have in mastering [these names]."

Because of these objections, most of the avenues have retained their numerical designations. But the vast majority of the Committee's recommendations were accepted. About 200 street name changes took effect, although approximately one-half were concerned merely with replacing "avenue" with "street" or eliminating "south" from a number of avenues.

The fourth period in street naming took place after World War I and lasted approximately two decades. Here we find private developers—as opposed to public officials—remembering and honoring the City's Spanish heritage. Spanish-sounding street names were selected by realty companies because such names carried an assumed mark of distinction. San

Francisco's developers and contractors have consistently requested that the Board of Supervisors name streets for their friends or relatives, but especially for whatever they considered popular and thus marketable.

In the last few years, however, another strong trend has emerged. Because of the City's changing ethnic composition, many Irish and English street names, names that don't have the same resonance for the newer settlers of Asian or Hispanic heritage, are being changed: Labor leader Cesar Chavez has been memorialized with a street that has replaced Army Street, and Lefty O'Doul has become Tandang Sora to remember a Philippine patriot, while South Drive has been changed to Martin Luther King, Jr. Drive to honor the slain civil-rights leader. Though some people may bemoan the passing of the likes of Lefty (there is still a bridge named after him), they should remember that street names will, and should, change with the times, as the city they describe and make understandable changes. And there has never been a city of such glorious and rapid change as San Francisco.

Louis K. Loewenstein
San Francisco
October, 1995

CITY STREET NAMES A-Z

ACADIA Street: Probably named for France's Atlantic seaboard possessions in North America during the 17th and 18th centuries. In turn, Acadia derives from Arcadia, a mountainous district of ancient Greece thought of as the ideal region of rural contentment. The North American Acadia included parts of Quebec, Maine, Nova Scotia, and the other maritime provinces of Canada.

ACEVEDO Avenue: Luis Joaquin Alvarez de Acevedo was an early settler.

AERIAL Way: An appropriate name for a street on top of Sunset Heights. At 700 feet, this hill is the fourth highest in the city. Mt. Davidson is the highest at 938 feet, followed by Mt. Sutro (918 feet) and Twin Peaks (903 and 910 feet).

AGNON Way: Brother Agnon Aviani was a faculty member of St. Mary's College from 1877 to 1934. This street is situated near the former site of this school's campus, now just west of St. Mary's Recreation Center. St. Mary's, a Christian Brothers facility, occupied this location from 1863 until 1889.

AGUA Way: The Spanish word for "water" is an appropriate name for this street, since it abuts Stanford Heights reservoir.

AHERN Way: Francis J. Ahern was chief of police for two years beginning in 1956.

ALABAMA Street: The state was named for the river of the same name. These words came from an Indian tribe whose name was derived from the Choctaw words *alba*, meaning "thicket" or "plants," and *amo*, meaning "reapers" or "plant reapers."

ALADDIN Terrace: This thoroughfare was probably named for the Arabic boy Aladdin, who discovered a genie in an oil lamp. Mark Twain, writing in the *Alta California* in 1866, said of San Francisco, "She is the new Aladdin who shall seize [the lamp] from its obscurity and summon the genie and command him to crown her . . . ."

ALAMEDA Street: *Alameda* is the Spanish word for "poplar grove," derived from *alamo*, which means "poplar tree." The street was named after the county in the East Bay.

ALBATROSS Court: The albatross, the world's largest seabird, inhabits only the oceans of the southern hemisphere.

ALBION Street: This was the Romans' name for England. Albion is derived from the Latin word *albion*, which means "white." When English explorer Sir Francis Drake first came to northern California in 1579, he called the area Nova Albion, or New England.

ALDRICH Alley: Mark Aldrich (1801–1873) has the distinction of being one of three persons whose first and last names or whose two last names are used separately to name two different streets. He is joined by General Winfield Scott and Captain Fernando Rivera y Moncada. The street that bears Aldrich's given name is Mark Lane. Although Aldrich's life was colorful, no one knows why he was so honored. Born in New York, he moved to Illinois and was elected to the state legislature in 1836. In 1845, in the town of Nauvoo, Illinois, he was tried and acquitted of murdering the visionary founder of the Mormons, Joseph Smith, and Smith's brother Hyrum, as well as of wounding follower John Taylor. Aldrich deserted his family in 1850 and headed for the Gold Rush.

ALEMANY Boulevard: Archbishop Joseph S. Alemany, first archbishop of San Francisco, was born in Spain. After serving as the Bishop of Monterey (1850–1853), Alemany came north, where he held his post in San Francisco for 31 years. Although he became an American citizen, he eventually returned to Valencia, Spain, where he died in 1888.

ALHAMBRA Street: Moorish fortress and palace in the Andalusian region of southern Spain. In Arabic, *alhambra* meant "The Red," referring to the color of the fortress walls.

ALLEN Street: A Scottish contractor, born in the town of Natick, Allen sailed around Cape Horn and headed for the Gold Rush of 1849. He built the first homes on Leavenworth and Hyde streets (see also Natick Street).

ALMA Street: *Alma,* the Spanish word for "soul" is also a woman's name. The name probably honored a pioneer.

ALOHA Avenue: The all-purpose Hawaiian word for "hello," "goodbye" and "love." In the late 1920s Hawaii was a popular tourist mecca, and this street, which was built in this period, was named to take advantage of this allure.

ALPHA Street: From the first letter of the Greek alphabet. Alpha is near Delta street, but neither Beta nor Gamma street exists.

ALPINE Terrace: Derived from the European mountain range, "alpine" is an appropriate appellation for a street on lofty (510 feet) Corona Heights.

ALTA Street: The Spanish adjective for "high" is a favorite California place name. Alta Street is near the top of Telegraph Hill.

ALTA MAR Way: The Spanish words *alta mar* mean "high sea." Overlooking both the Pacific Ocean and the Bay, Alta Mar is located in the extreme northwestern part of the City, one block south of Lincoln Park and one block east of Sutro Heights Park.

ALTA VISTA Terrace: Spanish for "high view." This short street on the slopes of Russian Hill offers an attractive panorama of the City and the Bay.

ALVARADO Street: Juan B. Alvarado was the twelfth governor of Mexican California, from 1836 to 1842. A central figure in California's history, along with Pio Pico and José Castro, he led the opposition to the American occupation. The geographical center of San Francisco is on the east side of Grandview Avenue between 23rd and Alvarado streets.

ALVISO Street: Corporal Domingo Alviso and his family of five accompanied Juan Bautista de Anza in 1776.

AMADOR Street: José Maria Amador (1794–1883), a native of San Francisco, was a soldier at the San Francisco Presidio as a young man. He then became the major domo of Mission San Jose. At age 49, he was granted Rancho San Ramon, a large land tract.

AMAZON Avenue: Ancient Greeks believed a race of female warriors lived on the western fringe of the world. After Francisco de Orellana first navigated this Brazilian river, he claimed he had fought with skillful women warriors, the Amazons of legend, hence the name of the river. The river's length is second only to the Nile's, and the area drained by the Amazon River is twice as large as the drainage area of the Congo River, the Amazon's closest competitor in drainage.

AMBROSE BIERCE Street: (formerly Aldrich Alley) Ambrose Bierce was an iconoclastic and uncompromising columnist on the *San Francisco Examiner* (1887–1896). He is most admired today for his *Devil's Dictionary*, his macabre supernatural tales, and his exceedingly realistic Civil War stories. At the age of 71 he went to Mexico with the vague idea of joining Pancho Villa and was never seen again.

AMHERST Street: Named after the New England college, which was named for Lord Jeffrey Amherst, a British general who fought in the French and Indian War.

ANDERSON Street: Possibly named for Robert Anderson, a Union General during the Civil War.

ANDOVER Street: Probably named after the town in Massachusetts, which was named after a town in Hampshire, England, either of which may have been the home town of several of San Francisco's original settlers.

ANNA Lane: A popular, but unverified story, tells that two brothers with the name of Lane were to divide a piece of land with the flip of a coin.

The winner was to receive the choice of halves while the loser got the other half plus the privilege of naming the street along its western boundary. The loser chose his daughter's name, Anna.

ANNAPOLIS Terrace: The capital city of Maryland was originally named Anne Arundell Town after the wife of Cecil Calvert, the Baron of Baltimore and founder of the colony of Maryland. The name of the town was changed to Annapolis to honor England's Princess Anne, who later became Queen Anne, the last Stuart monarch. *Polis* is the Greek word for "city."

ANNE LARSEN Lane: A fitting name for a street in St. Francis Square, which is a housing project sponsored by the International Longshoremen's Union, located on the Geary Expressway between Webster and Laguna streets. The *Anne Larsen* was a three-masted schooner of 376 tons and 48,000 board feet capacity.

ANNIE Street: There are two possible origins for this name. First, and more likely, is that it was named by surveyor William the name was chosen by early settler Immanuel Charles Christian Eddy for Jasper O'Farrell's boat. The other possibility is that the name was chosen by early settler Immanuel Charles Christian Russ to honor a daughter.

ANTHONY Street: The maiden name of Mrs. William Eddy, whose husband was the city surveyor in 1849.

ANZA Street: (Also Boulevard) In 1775, at the age of 40, Captain Juan Bautista de Anza, the "Father of San Francisco," led a sizable party of soldiers and settlers from Sonora, Mexico, north to Monterey. The journey was slower than had been anticipated, and Anza was obligated to return to Mexico to oversee his administrative responsibilities. Lieutenant José Moraga, second in command, continued on to San Francisco Bay, arriving on July 27, 1776. Most of Anza's party of 240 soldiers, priests, and settlers remained. They located a site for their mission on the shores of what had been named La Laguna de Nuestra Señora de los Dolores, and also selected a site for the Presidio near the present Fort Point.

ANZA VISTA Avenue: Spanish for "view of, or by, Anza"; Anza Vista is also the name of the neighborhood through which this street runs. Perhaps Captain Anza's party stopped here to view the Bay on their original exploration of this area. The group camped about one-half mile away on the evening of March 27, 1776.

APOLLO Street: Apollo was the Greek god of the sun, constitutions, prophecy, crops, and the arts.

APPAREL Way: At one time, this thoroughfare ran through the center of "Apparel City," but now all the clothing manufacturers have moved away from this industrial area located just east of the intersection of Highways 101 and 280.

APTOS Avenue: Rancho de Aptos was a Spanish land grant for which the community of Aptos was named. The name is probably the Spanish rendering of a local Costanoan Indian word.

AQUAVISTA Way: *Aqua* is Latin for "water," and vista is Spanish for "view." From this street, almost at the top of Twin Peaks, the Pacific Ocean is just visible over the rooftops.

ARBALLO Drive: Señora Feliciana Arballo accompanied the Anza party. She brought her two daughters, Tomasa and Estaquio, along on the journey to San Francisco.

ARCH Street: Possibly named after Arch Street in Philadelphia or for an underwater rock in the Bay that was blown up on August 15, 1901.

ARCO Way: *Arco* is Spanish for "arch" or "bow."

ARDATH Court: Ardath Nichols, a prominent community leader in Hunters Point during the 1960s, was honored by having a street named for him.

ARELLANO Avenue: Manuel Ramirez Arellano, a soldier under Captain Juan Anza, was born in 1742 in Puebla, Mexico. He arrived in what became San Francisco with Anza's company in 1776.

ARGENT Alley: The French word for "silver" or "money."

ARGONAUT Avenue: According to the Greek myth, Jason and the Argonauts were the strong sailors of the ship *Argo* who sought the fabled Golden Fleece. During the expedition, the hardy adventurers struggled against the elements as well as against other men. The early settlers of San Francisco, nicknamed Argonauts, struggled to survive in their quest to obtain California's fabulous gold.

ARGUELLO Boulevard: José Darío Argüello, the Spanish-born commander of the Presidio, was the governor of Alta California in 1814. He is buried in the cemetery at Mission Dolores. His son, Luís Antonio, was California's first nativeborn governor. He was the second governor under the Mexican flag (1822–25) and a commander of the Presidio.

ARKANSAS Street: Named for the state and the river, which in turn were named for the *Quapaw* tribe of the Sioux, who called themselves *Ugakhpah*, "downstream people."

ARMISTEAD Road: General Lewis Addison Armistead commanded the Presidio in 1859. He was killed in the Battle of Gettysburg while fighting for the Confederacy.

ARMSTRONG Avenue: General Samuel Strong Armstrong was the founder of Hampton Institute in HamptonSydney, Virginia, one of the first American institutions of higher learning for blacks. Armstrong was instrumental in helping Booker T. Washington complete his formal education.

ARROYO Way: The Spanish word *arroyo* means "stream" or "creek." It is possible that a small stream once ran nearby.

ARTHUR Avenue: Born in 1831, Chester A. Arthur was the twenty-first President of the United States (1881–1885). He assumed the office after the assassination of James A. Garfield.

ASHBURY Street: (Also Terrace) Munroe Ashbury served as a member of the Board of Supervisors for the fifth ward from 1864 to 1870. He was instrumental in the creation of Golden Gate Park.

ATALAYA Terrace: The Spanish word *atalaya* means "watchtower" or "lookout."

AVALON Avenue: In Celtic mythology, Avalon was "the land of the blessed." It was assumed to be the earthly paradise where enchantress Morgan le Fay healed King Arthur. Prior to 1907, this street was called Japan Street.

AVILA Street: Named after both the Spanish province and its capital, the city of Avila, which has been called the "finest medieval remnant in Spain" because of the preservation of the walls which were constructed in the 12th Century and at that time completely surrounded the City.

AVON Way: *Avon* is Celtic for "river" or "water." Several rivers and a county in England bear the name.

AZTEC Street: The Aztec tribe's name is probably derived from the Aztec word *aztlán*, which means "white land." The Aztecs believed they had been created in Aztlan (probably northwestern Mexico and southwestern United States), where they dwelt before moving to central Mexico. In the 13th Century they settled in the Valley of Mexico, now Mexico City. Aztlan was also an early name for California. The adjacent street, Montezuma, is named for the leader of the Aztecs during the Spanish conquest of Mexico.

BADEN Street: Named after a stop on either the San Francisco-San Jose Railroad or the seashore excursion line, which some old timers called "the peanut special." Near this station was the Baden dog-racing track. *Baden* is German for "bath", "spa," or "hot springs."

BAKER Street: (Also Court) Colonel Edward Dickinson Baker arrived in San Francisco from Illinois in 1852. One of the City's foremost lawyers, he was noted for his ability as an orator. After he delivered a persuasive speech in the park that thereafter became known as Union Square, Baker was credited with bringing California into the Union. His most famous defense was of a gambler, Charles Cora, who had been accused of murdering Marshal William Richardson in a saloon. Baker argued that the bonds between prostitute Belle Ryan, whom Richardson had allegedly insulted, and her lover Cora were as legitimate as any other between a man and a woman. He termed it, "A tie which angels might not blush to approve." The jury at the trial was so convinced by his persuasive appeal (and the admittedly provocative personality of Richardson, a crony of corrupt politicians and gamblers) that they wavered between verdicts of manslaughter and murder. In the interim, the Vigilance Committee grabbed Cora and another accused murderer from the jail and hanged them in front of an angry crowd. Later, Baker, a great friend of Abraham Lincoln, was killed in the Civil War battle of Ball's Bluff. He is buried in the Presidio. The geographical center of San Francisco (land and water combined) is to be found at the southwest corner of Fulton and Baker streets.

BALANCE Street: The timbers of the sailing ship *Balance* were discovered on the site of this downtown street during excavations. It is a tiny alley (perhaps the shortest in the city.)

BALBOA Street: Vasco Nuñez de Balboa (1475–1519) discovered the Pacific Ocean. On September 25, 1513, after crossing the Isthmus of Panama and climbing a hill near the Gulf of San Miguel, Balboa saw what he called the "South Sea." King Ferdinand, impressed by Balboa's achievements, named him governor of Panama and the Pacific. Five years later, a rival accused him on spurious charges of treason. Balboa was convicted, and beheaded in January 1519.

BALDWIN Court: James Baldwin, novelist, short story writer, and playwright, wrote *Go Tell It On the Mountain, Notes of a Native Son*, and *Nobody Knows My Name*. As a spokesman for African-Americans and civil rights, Baldwin was honored with a street named for him in predominantly Black Hunters Point in the 1960s.

BALTIMORE Way: The Maryland city was named after the Irish barony of Baltimore, the seat of the Calvert family, the founders of the colony of Maryland. Cecil Calvert, the second Baron of Baltimore was the founder of the catholic colony. His father, George Calvert had wanted to establish a colony that would be a sanctuary for practicing Roman Catholics and asked for a charter for such a colony in the Chesapeake Bay area. The charter was granted in 1632, two months after George Calvert's death, and Cecil Calvert became the first proprietor of the colony of Maryland.

BANCROFT Avenue: In 1856, Hubert Howe Bancroft (1832–1918) opened a bookstore in San Francisco, the biggest of its kind west of Chicago. As a special project, Bancroft started to collect books on California and the West. His collection had grown to 60,000 volumes by 1905, when he sold them to the University of California for $250,000! Bancroft was also renowned for his histories, which totaled more than 40 volumes, concerned primarily with the West. He and a host of assistants compiled, wrote, and edited these works between 1869 and 1890.

BANKS Street: Possibly named after Nathaniel P. Banks, a Union general during the Civil War. Before the Civil War, he was a prominent congressman and governor of Massachusetts; after the war, he returned to Congress. Starting in 1853, he served in ten Congresses, although not continuously. During the war, he fought several engagements against Stonewall Jackson—Banks won at Kernstown, but lost at Cedar Mountain.

BANNAM Place: John Bannan was an Irish pioneer and brewer. According to Herb Caen, when the City put up an official street sign in 1858, it read Bannam, and nobody has ever bothered to correct the typographical mistake.

BANNEKER Terrace: Benjamin Banneker was a black surveyor who assisted Major L'Enfant in laying out Washington, D.C.

BANNOCK Street: Probably named after the Great Basin Indian tribe. The Bannocks were never numerous and probably consisted of not more than 2,000 people at any one time. By 1900, only about 500 Bannocks remained.

BARCELONA Avenue: The Spanish city was founded by the ancient Carthaginians. Its name may be derived from the famous ruling Carthage family, the Barcas.

BARNARD Avenue: Major General A. C. Barnard was one of the officers in charge of fortifying San Francisco's harbor in 1854. These installations included batteries at Fort Point, Alcatraz Island, and Lime Rock Point.

BARTLETT Street: Lieutenant Washington A. Bartlett was the first United States citizen to serve under Spanish rule as "first officer" of Yerba Buena, beginning January 30, 1847. He proclaimed the official name of the city to be San Francisco and also designated Washington, Clay, and Montgomery streets.

BARTOL Street: Abraham Bartol, an early settler, was president of the Board of Assistant Aldermen in 1850.

BATTERY Street: Originally named Sloat Street, the name of this street was changed to commemorate one of the City's early fortifications, a battery of cannons taken from the Presidio in 1847 and then erected on Clark's Point by Lt. J. S. Misroon. Misroon, a member of Captain Montgomery's landing party in 1846, raised the American flag in the Presidio thus closing the Mexican period in the City's history. The Clark's Point stronghold, situated near the foot of Vallejo Street, was originally called Fort Montgomery.

BATTERY BLANEY Road: This road leads to Battery Blaney in the Presidio. It was named to honor Lieutenant Blaney, an artillery officer and a Spanish-American War hero.

BATTERY CAULFIELD Road: Lieutenant Col. Thomas Caulfield died at Letterman General Hospital in March 1955, after serving forty-four years in the artillery.

BAY Street: Named after the Bay itself, which this street once abutted.

BAY VIEW Street: There is a view of the Bay from the western edge of the street. This is also the name of the neighborhood that offers a splendid view, in places, of the Bay.

BAYSHORE Boulevard: This road once ran along the shore of the Bay, which has since moved east because of infilling.

BEACH Street: The beach once came up to this street. Because of landfill, this street is now one block from the beach in the Fisherman's Wharf area of North Beach.

BEALE Street: Edward F. Beale, a naval officer in the Mexican War, brought camels to California hoping to use them for long-haul transportation. The experiment failed. Later, Beale became surveyor general of California and, subsequently, US ambassador to Austria.

BEATRICE Lane: Beatrice Dunbar was an important community activist in the 1960s at Hunters Point.

BEAUMONT Avenue: This French word means "beautiful mountain." It is appropriate for a street that runs to and from Lone Mountain.

BELDEN Street: Josiah Belden, who was born in Connecticut, came to California with the first overland emigrant party in 1841. He became a rancher, a merchant, and the first mayor of San Jose.

BELLA VISTA Way: These Spanish words mean "beautiful view." At one time, this street, high atop the slopes of Mt. Davidson, had a beautiful view of the southern part of San Francisco and of San Bruno Mountain. Now homes block this view.

BELLE Avenue: Although the specific source of this name is unknown, it is possible that it is a remembrance of one of the more notorious ladies of early San Fancisco, such as Belle Star or Belle Ryan. Even though this name means "beautiful," this street is anything but beautiful, since it's positioned between two freeways.

BELVEDERE Street: Italian for "look-out" or "viewpoint," but there is no significant view to be seen from it.

BEMIS Street: Probably named to honor a person named Bemis who fed the homeless after the 1906 earthquake and fire.

BENNINGTON Street: A battle in the Revolutionary War took place near the town of the Bennington in southwestern Vermont. The town was probably named after Bennington Wentworth (1696–1770), Colonial governor of New Hampshire (1741–67), who encouraged settlement in what is now Vermont. He was a founder of Dartmouth College in New Hampshire. Another theory is that the name came from Bennington, Hertfordshire, England.

BERGEN Alley: Probably named after the port city in Norway, which was that country's capital in the 12th and 13th centuries.

BERKELEY Way: Bishop George Berkeley was an Irish prelate and philosopher (1685–1753). His quotation, "Westward the course of empire takes its way," inspired Frederick Billings to name the East Bay town of Berkeley after him. Berkeley's treatise *De Motu* anticipated Einstein when it refuted accepted Newtonian physics.

BERKSHIRE Way: Named for Berkshire county in England. *Berk* is a British (and Welsh) term meaning "top" or "summit."

BERNAL HEIGHTS Boulevard: Probably named for Cornelio de Bernal, who acquired the entire territory of what was to become Bernal Rancho from Governor Jimeo Castro in 1839.

BERNICE Street: Possibly named for a friend or relative of a pioneer.

BERRY Street: Richard N. Berry, born in Massachusetts, was a pioneer merchant who emigrated to the Bay Area in 1849.

BERTHA Lane: Bertha Freeman was a wellknown Hunters Point community leader in the 1960s when the Redevelopment Agency housing project was in the planning stage.

BERTIE MINOR Lane: This is an appropriate name for a street in a housing project sponsored by the International Longshoremen's Union. The *Bertie Minor* was a three-masted schooner built in 1864, that carried cargoes of copra and petroleum products.

BLACKSTONE Court: Nathaniel Blackstone was a merchant and a member of the Vigilance Committee of 1856. This tiny alley is situated on a trail that ran from the financial district to the Presidio in the 1860's. Blackstone is the City's smallest officially designated historic district.

BLAKE Street: Prior to 1882, this street was called Ferrie street Since Maurice C. Blake was mayor of San Francisco during that year, the street was probably named for him.

BLANCHE Street: This French word means "white," and it was a common woman's name. The street was probably named for a friend or relative of a pioneer.

BLUXOME Street: Isaac J. Bluxome, Jr., a prominent businessman, commanded a group of vigilantes in 1849. He was secretary of both the 1851 and 1856 Vigilance Committees.

BOALT Street: John Henry Boalt, an Ohioan, originally worked as a mining and mechanical engineer. At the end of the Civil War, Boalt came west and he opened an assaying business in Austin, Nevada in 1865. He preferred, however, the law and was appointed a judge later in the decade. He moved to the Bay Area in 1871 and practiced law in San Francisco until 1895, although he lived in Oakland. His widow donated $100,000 to the University of California School of Law in Berkeley, which is now named Boalt Hall.

BOARDMAN Place: Possibly named after W. F. Boardman, a prominent surveyor in the 1860s. He surveyed a great deal of Alameda County.

BOB KAUFMAN Street: (formerly Harwood Alley) Bob Kaufman (1925–1986), a legendary poet was known in France as the American Rimbaud. At one time Kaufman lived in an apartment located in a building at the intersection of this alley and Filbert Street.

BONIFACIO Street: Bonifacio was a hero of the Philippine struggle against the Spanish in the 1890s. To honor him, the name of one of the three blocks of Shipley Street was changed to Bonifacio Street in 1979.

BONITA Street: This is the Spanish word for "pretty."

BONVIEW Street: This street was originally called Buena Vista Street. To avoid confusion with Buena Vista Terrace and Avenue, the name was changed. Both Buena Vista and Bonview mean "good view"; the former is Spanish and the latter is a combination of French and English. (See Buena Vista Avenue.)

BORICA Street: Diego de Borica was governor of California from 1794 to 1800. This thoroughfare was named in 1909 by the Street Name Commission, which said of Borica that he was "able, honest, and conscientious."

BOSTON SHIP Plaza: The remains of a merchant ship with this name were found in Yerba Buena Cove. This plaza is the present site of the Golden Gateway complex. Before the Gold Rush of 1849 New England merchants exchanged Yankee notions with the local residents—Californios as they were called—for hides and tallow, which were then shipped around Cape Horn and back to Boston. The leather was made into shoes, which were often shipped back to the West Coast.

BOSWORTH Street: The De Boom family once owned the tract of land in Glen Park where this street is located. Romain De Boom named this street for a family friend.

BOWDOIN Street: The college in Maine was named for James Bowdoin, a political leader in Massachusetts during the American Revolution and the first president of the American Academy of Arts and Sciences, which he founded in 1790. His academic disciplines were physics and astronomy.

BOWLING GREEN Drive: Named for the game of lawn bowling, which is played in the outdoor court next to this street in Golden Gate Park.

BOYLSTON Street: The street in Boston was probably named for Zabdiel Boylston (1679–1766), a Massachusetts physician who introduced smallpox inoculations to America.

BRADY Street: Probably named for an early real-estate dealer. Until recently the part of the City where this street is located was called "Irish Town"; it is now known as "South of Market."

BRANNAN Street: Samuel Brannan was the leader of a group of Mormons who sailed into Yerba Buena on July 31, 1846. A jack-of-all-trades, Brannan started the City's first newspaper, The California Star; led the first vigilante group; announced the discovery of gold at Sutter's Mill; and sent the first gold nuggets to the Atlantic Coast. Brannan also performed the first marriage and preached the first sermon to occur in this community under American rule.

BRAZIL Avenue: The largest country in South America was named by the Portuguese for the brazil tree, a red-colored tree common in the country. The bark was used by the Indians who lived in the northeastern part of Brazil to color their bodies for ceremonial functions.

BREEN Place: Patrick Breen was one of the 45 survivors of the Donner party, an ill-fated group of emigrants who attempted to cross the Sierra Nevada during the winter of 1846–47. Fierce, early winter storms blocked the emigrants in their attempts to reach the western side of the mountains. Some members of the Donner party resorted to cannabalism to survive. Breen wrote a record of the ordeal, Diary of the Donner Party.

BRET HARTE Terrace: Easterner Bret Harte—tutor, stagecoach messenger, typesetter, newspaper reporter, novelist, and poet—came to San Francisco in 1854 and wrote about the Gold Rush and the pioneers. His most famous stories are "The Luck of Roaring Camp" and "The Outcasts of Poker Flat."

BRIDGE VIEW Drive: This street does have a view of the San Francisco-Oakland Bay Bridge as well as a tower of the Golden Gate Bridge.

BRITTON Street: Joseph Britton was a wellknown San Francisco-based lithographer and a friend of Henry Schwerin, who developed the subdivision in Visitacion Valley in which this street is located.

BROAD Street: Possibly named after the Philadelphia street which Philadelphians incorrectly consider to be the longest straight street in the United States. Its twelve-mile length, however, is exceeded by Chicago's 23-mile Western Avenue, which is the longest straight-away in the United States, if not the world.

BROADWAY: The famous New York street acquired its name because of its width. The original name, which the Dutch settlers gave to this thoroughfare in what was then New Amsterdam, was "Breetweg."

BRODERICK Street: New York-born David C. Broderick was a San Francisco realestate investor, who was elected to the state senate in 1850. Under Broderick, the "Tammany Democracy," which was the strongest political organization in the City, flourished. Subsequently, he became a US Senator. At Lake Merced on September 13, 1859, he lost his life in a duel with David Terry, a recently resigned Chief Justice of the California Supreme Court. The quarrel centered on control of the Democratic party in California, with Terry calling Broderick a traitor at the party's state convention.

BROOKLYN Place: Probably named after the ship that brought Mormon emigrants from the East Coast to San Francisco before the Gold Rush. The story goes that the 200 Mormons who landed in 1846, doubled the City's population. In turn, it is likely that the Brooklyn was named for the eastern town, now a borough of New York City, which was named after a community in Holland.

BROOKS Street: Colonel Horace Brooks was the commanding officer of the Presidio from November 1872 to January 1877. He died at the age of 84 in 1894.

BROSNAN Street: Charles W. Brosnan, a native of Ireland, came overland from New York to California in 1850. He practiced law in California for twelve years; then he moved to Nevada, where he became the first chief justice of the Nevada Supreme Court. Serving only a few years, he returned to California to die in San Jose in 1867.

BROTHERHOOD WAY: This is a unique highway and private street owned by the religious institutions that line its path. These include the St.

Thomas More Catholic Church, Congregation Beth Israel-Judea, the Lake Merced Church of Christ, the Holy Trinity Greek Orthodox Church, and St. Gregory, an Armenian church, as well as the Richmond Masonic Temple and the Brandeis-Hillel Day School. Prior to 1958, the street was called Stanley Drive, but after these diverse buildings were constructed, the ecumenical spirit prevailed and the name was changed.

BRUSSELS Street: The Belgian capital is situated on the Senne River. At the point where the river and a road crossed, a community arose in the middle ages. The residents called it *Bruoc-della*, which means the "settlement in the marshes."

BRYANT Street: Edwin Bryant served as *alcalde* (mayor) of San Francisco in 1847. A prominent San Francisco property holder, he took an active interest in politics. Bryant favored the sale of beach and water lots to raise money for the city treasury. He also invoked the Mexican law that gave governors of territories the power to make land grants.

BUCARELI Drive: It was Lieutenant General Baylio Brother Antonio Maria de Bucareli y Ursua, Viceroy of New Spain, who sent Captain Juan de Anza north in 1774 to establish a Presidio and a mission. He was very interested in the little community of Yerba Buena and envisioned a great commercial city by the Bay.

BUCHANAN Street: John C. Buchanan, auctioneer and real-estate investor, was a prominent local politician. In 1847, he became the chief magistrate under mayors Bryant and Hyde.

BUCKINGHAM Way: The English market town and borough on the River Ouse was the site of a Roman settlement and later an important anti-Norman Conquest stronghold.

BUENA VISTA Avenue: (Also Terrace) Although Spanish for "good view," the name came from the Battle of Buena Vista during the Mexican-American War, in which General Winfield Scott became a hero.

BURKE Avenue: Edmund Burke was an English statesman and political thinker who was prominent in the British government from 1765 to about 1795. Important in the history of political thought, his policies called for a conciliatory attitude toward the American colonies and for steps to ease the economic and political oppression of Ireland.

BURNETT Avenue: Peter H. Burnett was the first elected Governor of California, in 1849. In 1851, he returned to the practice of law and later he served as a justice on the California Supreme Court.

BURNS Place: Probably named for a pioneer, several of whom had the last name of Burns.

BURR Avenue: George Burr was general manager and chief engineer of the San Francisco Water Department in the early 1960s.

BUSH Street: There are at least four possible origins: 1) Bush Street in Philadelphia. The name was selected by Swiss surveyor and sailor, Jean Jacques Vioget, who mapped San Francisco's streets in 1839. 2) J. P. Bush, one of Jasper O'Farrell's assistants. O'Farrell succeeded Vioget as the city engineer. 3) Doctor J. P. Bush, an early pioneer. 4) According to an 1897 issue of the authoritative Pioneer Magazine of San Jose, "Bush Street was not named for anyone. As a small boy in San Francisco, the late Rear Admiral R. W. Meade carried the chain that the surveyors used to measure the streets. Each street had been named until they came to this street. When the surveyor asked, 'What shall we call this one?' Young Meade, pointing to a bush that had been causing them trouble, remarked, 'Why not call it Bush Street?' And Bush Street it was called."

CABRILLO Street: The navigator Juan Rodriguez Cabrillo is considered to be the discoverer of Alta California. He entered San Diego Bay on September 28, 1542. In the following November, Cabrillo was the first sailor to cruise the Pacific as far north as the Russian River.

CALEDONIA Street: The ancient Romans' name for an area of north Britain beyond Roman control, roughly corresponding to what is now Scotland. A club with this name existed in San Francisco in the 1860s, which may have been the inspiration for the street's name.

CALGARY Street: Probably named after the city in Alberta, Canada. Calgary is Gaelic for "clear running water." This town began as a Northwest Mounted Police post, which was named Fort Calgary in 1876.

CALHOUN Terrace: John Caldwell Calhoun (1782–1850), a political leader from South Carolina, held the offices of US congressman, Secretary of War, Secretary of State, US senator, and Vice-President. He was an articulate champion of states' rights and a symbol of the Old South.

CALIFORNIA Street: According to Michael Venega, a Mexican Jesuit and author, writing in the early 1700s, "This name owed its origin to some accident; possibly to some words spoken by Indians, and misunderstood by the Spaniards." A more likely possibility is that it first appeared in the novel *The Adventures of Esplandián*, written by García Ordóñez de Montalvo and published in Toledo, Spain, in 1521. In the novel, California was the name of a fabulous island in the Pacific, rich in minerals and precious stones and the home of a tribe of Amazons, who were ruled by Queen Califia.

CAMBON Drive: Brother Pedro Benito Cambón, a Franciscan religious official with Captain Anza's party, was assigned to Mission Dolores by Father Junípero Serra in 1776.

CAMBRIDGE Street: Named after the University town in England located on the river Cam.

CAMELLIA Avenue: This plant is a type of evergreen shrub native to East Asia and notable for its colorful and attractive flowers.

CAMERON Way: Donaldina Cameron, born in New Zealand in 1869, arrived two years later in San Francisco. For many years her Chinese Presbyterian Mission at the corner of Sacramento and Joice streets was a haven for Chinese girls who had been sold into prostitution. She died in 1968 at the age of 99.

CAMP Street: This is the location of the first encampment of Captain Anza's party in 1776. It consisted of a row of tents and shacks about 500 yards east of the present site of Mission Dolores.

CAPISTRANO Avenue: Named for Mission San Juan Capistrano, located just north of the town of San Clemente. Saint John Capistran was a fighting priest of the 15th Century who played a heroic part in defending Vienna from the Turks.

CAPP Street: Probably named after a local realtor, Charles S. Capp, who was an early secretary of the San Francisco Real Estate Board.

CARDENAS Way: Juana Cardenas accompanied her husband, Felipe Santiago Tapia, a soldier with Captain Anza, to northern California in 1776. They had nine children which they brought along, and baptism records show that four more were born in Santa Clara after 1778.

CARGO Way: A street that leads to the piers where ships load and unload cargo.

CARMEL Street: The Carmelite Order was founded at Mt. Carmel in Palestine in the 12th Century. The mountain's Hebrew name is "Har Karmel" or "Ha-Karmel." This name dates back to biblical times and was derived from the Hebrew *kerem*, for "vineyard" or "orchard." In 1602, three friars of the Carmelite Order explored Monterey as members of Vizcaíno's expedition.

CAROLINA Street: The states—both North and South—were named for Caroline of Ansbach (1683–1737). As the wife of King George II, she was the Queen of Great Britain from 1727 to 1737.

CARROLL Avenue: Charles Carroll was the only Roman Catholic signer of the Declaration of Independence.

CARTER Street: Charles D. Carter was a land speculator and real-estate broker who published and edited the *San Francisco Real Estate Circular*. On May 25, 1871, he died of apoplexy at the age of 46.

CASA Way: The Spanish word *casa* means "house."

CASCADE Walk: Probably named for the mountain range, which extends north from northern California through Oregon and Washington and into British Columbia. The range was named for the great cascading waterfalls found along the Columbia River gorge on the Washington-Oregon border.

CASHMERE Street: Marcalee Cashmere was a prominent community leader in Hunters Point during the mid-Sixties, when the Redevelopment Agency's project there was in the planning stage.

CASITAS Avenue: Although there are houses of all sizes along this street, this Spanish word means "little houses."

CASSANDRA Court: She was the Greek mythological figure with whom Apollo fell in love. He proposed that if she gave herself to him, he would give her the gift of prophecy. She accepted the offer, received the gift, and then refused to give her favors. Apollo revenged himself by ordering that her prophecies should never be believed.

CASTELO Avenue: Gertrudis Castelo was the wife of Juan Antonio Vásquez, a soldier in Captain Anza's party of 1776.

CASTENADA Avenue: Castenada was a member of the Coronado expedition (1540–1542).

CASTILLO Street: The Spanish word *castillo* means "castle."

CASTLE Street: A street on Telegraph Hill adjacent to Windsor Alley. Windsor Castle has been one of the principal residences of the British royal family since the Ninth Century.

CASTRO Street: General José Castro was a descendant of a member of Captain Anza's original company. At one time, General Castro was in command of all the Spanish forces in California. Following the occupation of Monterey and San Francisco by American forces, he was a very active opponent to the rule of the United States.

CATHARINE Court: Probably named after a friend or relative of an early pioneer.

CAYUGA Avenue: Named after the Iroquois-speaking Indian tribe which originally inhabited central upstate New York.

CEDRO Avenue: This is the Spanish word for "cedar."

CENTRAL Avenue: This street runs through the approximate middle of San Francisco. Until 1904, Presidio Avenue was also called Central Avenue.

CERES Street: Named after the Roman goddess of agriculture.

CERRITOS Avenue: This Spanish word means "little hills" and is an appropriate name for a street located on one of San Francisco's numerous little hills.

CERVANTES Boulevard: Miguel de Cervantes (1547–1616) was an important Spanish author, novelist, playwright, and poet. His most famous work is *Don Quixote*.

CESAR CHAVEZ Street: (formerly Army Street) This recently renamed street honors labor leader Chavez. He was the founder of the United Farm Workers Union, an advocate of nonviolence, and the organizer of the 1965 table grapes boycott.

CHABOT Terrace: Anthony Chabot (1814–1888) was an early San Francisco capitalist and philanthropist. One of 16 children, Chabot was born in Quebec, Canada, and came to California to work in the gold mines near Nevada City. Called "the Father of Hydraulic Mining," Chabot was the first to mine gold by moving earth using water pressure. Later, Chabot built San Francisco's first public water system.

CHAIN OF LAKES Drive (East, West): This road in Golden Gate Park connects a chain of lakes known as North Lake, Middle Lake, and South Lake.

CHAPMAN Street: Possibly named for George H. Chapman, a Union general during the Civil War. During the Pennsylvania campaign, he led his regiment at Upperville, Gettysburg, Falling Waters, and Brandy Station. Wounded at a battle in Winchester, Virginia, Chapman recovered to fight in the Shenandoah campaign.

CHARLES J. BRENHAM Place: (formerly Seventh Street North) An early Mississippi riverboat captain, Charles J. Brenham, later commanded the S.S. *McKim* on its run between Sacramento and San Francisco. He was elected the second Mayor of San Francisco in 1851, and served two terms.

CHARLTON Court: Named, perhaps, after a dairy or a dairy owner. This cul-de-sac is reputed to have been a milk-wagon loading yard for a dairy that served the city a century ago and gave this district, Cow Hollow, its name.

CHARTER OAK Avenue: Probably named after Charter Oak Avenue in Hartford, Connecticut, famous for the oak tree that once shaded this eastern thoroughfare.

CHATTANOOGA Street: Chattanooga was a Civil War Battle near Chattanooga, Tennessee, in 1863. The city derives its name from an Indian expression for nearby Lookout Mountain.

CHESLEY Street: George W. Chesley was a pioneer who arrived in San Francisco on June 13, 1849. He was in the auction business for a year before moving to Sacramento to work as a mercantilist. From 1852 until 1854, Chesley was back in San Francisco, and he acquired and then subdivided the land where this street is located.

CHICAGO Way:. The origin of the name for the third largest city in the United States is controversial. The name is derived from any one of three Indian words meaning either "skunk," "wild onion," or "powerful."

CHILD Street: Originally called the Street of Good Children. The name was shortened by the 1909 Committee on Street Names.

CHRISTMAS TREE POINT Road: During the 1920s this street, high atop Twin Peaks, was the site of a huge Christmas tree that the City annually erected and lit there.

CHRISTOPHER Drive: George Christopher was the mayor of San Francisco for two terms (1956–1964). An inscription on his bust in City Hall states, "San Francisco was deep in his heart. He served our City with brilliant efficiency, devoted purpose and tireless devotion."

CHULA Lane: Today in Spanish this word means "low-class woman" while in early Spanish slang it meant "maiden" or "sensuous girl." Originally this lane was called Necropolis Street since it was located just outside a churchyard.

CHUMASERO Drive: Maria Angela Chumasero was married to a member of Captain Juan Anza's company, which arrived at the Bay in 1776.

CHURCH Street: Since Mission Dolores is only one block away, it is probably the namesake of this street.

CIELITO Drive: *Cielito* is Spanish for "darling." It is used as a term of endearment.

CIRCULAR Avenue: As the name suggests, this street curves; however, it does not make a complete circle.

CITYVIEW Way: A large part of the City may be seen from this street. All of the streets in this subdivision, Midtown Terrace, have names ending with the suffix "view."

CLAIRVIEW Court: In French, *clair* means "clear." This street is in the same subdivision as the previous entry.

CLARA Street: Probably named for a relative of a pioneer.

CLAREMONT Boulevard: The original source of the name for the Hotel Claremont in Berkeley and all other "Claremonts" is probably the Duke of Newcastle's country estate of the same name in England.

CLARENCE Place: Probably named after a friend or relative of a pioneer.

CLARENDON Avenue: The origin of this street name is uncertain. One explanation is that it was named for the first Earl of Clarendon, Edward Hyde (1609–1674). He was a famous lawyer, the historian of the "Great Rebellion," and the man who helped put Prince Charles back on the throne as Charles II. Another equally speculative opinion is that the street was named for the fourth Earl, George William Frederick Villiers (1800–1870), who served England twice as Foreign Secretary, the last time under Gladstone. A third version is that the street was named for a New England-born San Francisco pioneer named Addison Clarendon.

CLAY Street: A great orator and patriot, Henry Clay (1777–1852) was one of the most influential political leaders in the United States before the Civil War. His admirers called him "The Great Pacificator" and "The Great Compromiser." On August 2, 1873, San Francisco's first cable car ran down a sixblock stretch of Clay Street to Kearny Street. Clay, Washington, Montgomery, and Kearny are the street names that have been in use longer than any others in the City.

CLAYTON Street: Born in England, Charles C. Clayton (1825–1885) emigrated to America at the age of 17. Arriving in San Francisco in 1848, he became a quicksilver miner, then a gold miner. Returning to the City, he opened a flour and grain store. He climbed the political ladder, serving as a magistrate, assemblyman (1863–64), supervisor (1864–69), and congressman (1873–75). In his obituary, a newspaper stated, "The opinion became quite general that Mr. Clayton was caught trying to corner the barley market . . . and that his prospective losses produced the excitement which finally brought about the cerebral apoplexy. His friends in Oakland state that he was short on barley estimating his losses at about $25,000."

CLEARY Court: Don Cleary was the City's lobbyist in Sacramento during the 1960s when the Redevelopment Agency designed the Hunters Point project.

CLEMENT Street: New Yorker Roswell Percival Clement arrived in California in 1853. An attorney, Clement was a member of the Board of Supervisors from 1865 to 1867. The idea of extending Golden Gate Park west to the ocean is said to have been his. He was also the lawyer for the San Francisco Gas Light Company for about 18 years.

CLEMENTINA Street: Probably named after a pioneer. The name is derived from the Roman goddess who personified mercy and clemency.

CLEVELAND Street: Banker Charles T. Cleveland arrived in San Francisco in 1849.

CLIPPER Street and Terrace: An appropriate name for a street in this City, since the clipper ship was important in the early development of San Francisco. The necessity of carrying merchandise speedily to a distant market forced New England and New York ship builders and merchants to invent new and superior types of vessels. Hence, the clipper was designed with great length, sharp lines of entrance and clearance, and a flat bottom. These ships cut the time needed to sail from East Coast ports to San Francisco almost in half.

CLYDE Street: There are two possibilities for the origin of this street name: one explanation is that it was named after a pioneer, and the other is that it was named after the Clyde River in Scotland.

COLBY Street: Named after the college in Waterville, Maine, which was named for Gardner Colby, a Maine industrialist and textile manufacturer. He gave Waterville College $200,000, so the college's name was changed to honor its benefactor.

COLE Street: One possible source for this name is R. Beverly Cole, M.D., a San Francisco supervisor in the 1870s, who was instrumental in the formation of Golden Gate Park. Dr. Cole was the first president of the American Medical Association from the West Coast. Another possibility for the source of the street name is Cornelius Cole, a New York lawyer who arrived in San Francisco late in 1849. After a brief career mining gold, he practiced law in San Francisco and became one of the principal organizers of the City's Republican party. Cole was elected to the US House of Representatives in 1863 and to the US Senate in 1866. He died at the age of 102, the oldest person who had ever served as a Senator.

COLEMAN Street: William Tell Coleman, a prosperous merchant, was head of the Second Vigilance Committee in 1856. He is best remembered his testimony in court in favor of a merchant, Jansen, who had been beaten and robbed. Coleman's words encouraged the angry crowds, that were sympathetic to the mistreated merchant, to take the accused, Thomas Berdue, and lynch him along the waterfront. The military intervened before Berdue could be lynched. (See Jansen Street.)

COLIN P. KELLY JR. Street: Colin P. Kelly Jr. was the first American aviator to be killed during World War II. He died on December 9, 1941. On that day he dropped the first bomb to sink a Japanese warship, near the Philippine Islands. The street's name was changed from Japan Street to honor Kelly. The street's original name came from the street's proximity to the old Pacific Mail Steam Ship Company wharf, where boats headed for Japan docked.

COLLEGE Avenue and Terrace: Before St. Mary's College moved to Oakland, and later to its present location in Moraga, this street ran through the heart of the campus. The only evidence of the campus that remains are streets, which, on a map, have the composite shape of a bell. These streets were probably laid out in this fashion to represent the famed Bell(s) of St. Mary's.

COLON Avenue: This word is the Spanish form of "Columbus." It is the name of a province and a city in Panama, a district in Honduras, and a city in Cuba—all honoring Christopher Columbus.

COLTON Street: There are two possible origins. One possibility is C. O. Colton, a founder of the Southern Pacific Railway and an early associate of Huntington, Crocker, Stanford, and Hopkins. The other possible namesake is David Colton, the chief lawyer and financial director of the Central Pacific Railroad. He was also a second for David Broderick in his famous duel with David S. Terry. (See Broderick Street.)

COLUMBUS Avenue: Every year on or around October 12th, the discovery of America is reenacted in San Francisco's Aquatic Park.

COLUSA Place: This tribe of California Indians once lived along the west bank of the Sacramento River.

COMMER Court: Julia Commer was an important community activist in the 1960s at Hunters Point when the Redevelopment Agency's project there was being planned.

COMMERCIAL Street: An early, and at that time an important, street that ran from the stores and financial houses down to the wharves and piers along Kearny Street. Hence the name.

COMMONWEALTH Avenue: Probably named after Commonwealth Avenue in Boston, which may have gotten its name from the fact that Massachusetts (along with Virginia, Pennsylvania, and Kentucky) is a commonwealth rather than a state. In the 17th Century, the term was used by such writers as John Locke and Thomas Hobbes to mean an organized community.

COMPTON Road: In 1899, Brigadier General Charles E. Compton was the commanding officer of the Presidio for two short periods.

CONCORD Street: Probably named for the town in Massachusetts that is the site of the first skirmish of the American Revolution. Concord was the first Puritan settlement that was established inland. The name was inspired by the peaceful agreements the Puritans made with local Indians.

CONGO Street: Probably named for the world's second largest river basin (after the Amazon) and the second longest river in Africa (after the Nile). The name came from the Kongo people who inhabited central Africa; the Kingdom of Kongo was located on the lower part of the river's course, in what is now Zaire.

CONNECTICUT Street: The Connecticut River is the origin of the name for the colony and later the state. The word means "long river" and comes from the Mohican Indian word *quonehtacut* or *quinnehtukguet* or *connittecock*.

CONVERSE Street: Possibly named for Charles P. Converse, a colorful and rambunctious character who built the Millerton courthouse and jail near Friant in the San Joaquin Valley in 1867. He had the dubious distinction of being the first occupant of one of the cells in the jail after he got into a gun battle shortly after the construction was completed. Converse married the widow of a county treasurer who had mysteriously disappeared—along with a sizable amount of public funds—while on a trip with him. Eventually, Converse ran out of money himself and committed suicide.

CORA Street: Gambler Charles Cora killed US Marshal William Richardson in a saloon because of an alleged insult to Cora's lover, Belle Ryan. At the trial, Cora's lawyer, Colonel Baker (see Baker Street), argued that the ties between Cora and Ryan, a prostitute, were as strong as those of marriage. Reacting, a furious resident asked, "Has the man who thus endorsed the sinful union between gambler and prostitute, a mother living?" Cora was hanged by an angry mob on May 22, 1856. He is buried in the Mission Dolores cemetery next to Belle.

CORAL Road: Probably named after the stony skeletons of marine organisms.

CORBETT Avenue: This street is named for either one of two pioneers: William Corbett, who was an assistant supervisor under Mayor John W. Geary, from 1850–1851; or John Corbett, who was deputy county clerk to Thomas Hayes in the early 1850s.

CORDOVA Street: Possibly named after the English name for Córdoba, a Spanish city on the Guadalquivir River. It was the capital of Moslem Spain from the 8th to the 11th Century.

CORNWALL Street: Probably named after the region in the extreme southwest corner of England that was inhabited by Celtic Christians. It was the last part of England to submit to the Saxons and was not completely subjugated until the reign of Edward the Confessor (1042–66).

CORONA Street: The Spanish word for "crown" is derived from the Latin word for "wreath" or "circle."

CORONADO Street: Francisco Vasquez de Coronado (1510–1554) was a Spanish explorer of the North American Southwest whose expeditions resulted in the discovery of the Grand Canyon (1540). He failed to find the mythical treasure-laden cities of Cibola and Quivera that he was seeking.

CORTES Avenue: Hernán Cortés (1485–1547) was a Spanish conquistador who conquered both Cuba and Mexico by the time he was 36. He died in Spain after returning from a disastrous expedition to Honduras.

CORTLAND Avenue: Probably named for the town of Cortland in New York State.

COSO Avenue: The etymology of the word is uncertain. Some believe it to be a Shoshone Indian word that means "broken coal" or "burnt district."

COSTA Street: *Costa* is the Spanish word for "coast."

COTTAGE Row: Named for the cottages on this street that were acquired and improved by the Redevelopment Agency.

COUNTRY CLUB Drive: A street in Country Club Acres. This is a common name for a subdivision, but in this case there is no country club nearby.

COVENTRY Court: Probably named after the city and district of Coventry in the West Midlands of England.

CRAGMONT Avenue: There are no "crags" on this street near the top of Golden Gate Heights—and next to Rockridge Drive.

CRAGS Court: Probably named after the rock formation in adjoining Glen Canyon Park.

CRESPI Drive: Father Juan Crespí, a Franciscan priest, accompanied Gaspar de Portolá and Father Junípero Serra as they went north from San Diego to Monterey Bay, where in May 1770 they founded a mission and a fort near the ocean. In 1772, Father Crespí and Lieutenant Fages journeyed to the Berkeley hills looking for a practical land route to Point Reyes, but they were thwarted by San Pablo Bay. This expedition to the East Bay pre-dated Moraga's trip to San Francisco Bay by four years.

CRESTA VISTA Drive: Spanish for "view of the crest." It is possible to see Mt. Davidson from this street.

CRESTLINE Drive: This street approaches the crest of Twin Peaks.

CRESTMONT Drive: This street is so named because it is near the top of Mt. Sutro.

CRISSY FIELD Avenue: Crissy Field is the deactivated airstrip in the Presidio, which was named to honor Howard Dana Crissy, a captain in the U.S. Army and a veteran of World War I. Crissy was killed in his de Haviland aircraft during a transcontinental air race in 1921.

CROOKS Street: During the 1980s the residents considered changing this street's name because they thought the name reflected upon them unfavorably. However, the street was not named for an occupation, but rather to honor Matthew J. Crooks, an Irishman who landed in San Francisco in 1849. One year later he was elected a member of the Board of Supervisors. Unlike most pioneers, he died a wealthy man, with an estate in excess of a million dollars.

CULEBRA Terrace: This Spanish word means "snake," but this little alley is straight.

CUMBERLAND Street: Cumberland is a river and a city in western Maryland, whose names were taken from an old county in northwestern England. This was also the name of the Civil War army that was commanded by Robert Anderson and William Sherman, both of whom have streets in San Francisco named after them. These three street names reflect the patriotic pride that engulfed the City after the War between the States.

CUSTER Avenue: General George A. Custer, along with 250 soldiers under his command, was killed in a battle with Sioux Indians led by Chief Sitting Bull, near Montana's Little Big Horn River in 1876.

CYRIL MAGNIN Street: Known as "Mr. San Francisco," this former executive of the Joseph Magnin's stores was the City's chief of protocol and a distinguished civic figure in the 1970s and 80s.

DAKOTA Street: The state was named for the North American Plains Indians. The name Dakota means "allies."

DALEWOOD Way: One of a series of streets in a subdivision called Sherwood Forest, on the southern edge of Mt. Davidson Park. Another street in this area is Robin Hood Drive.

DARIEN Way: Probably named after the Isthmus of Darién (later Isthmus of Panama), site of the first attempted European settlement in South America: Santa Maria de la Antiqua del Darién. It was from this colony in Panama that Balboa made his famous trek to the Pacific in 1513. A subdivision called Balboa Terrace is traversed by this street.

DARTMOUTH Street: Dartmouth College in New Hampshire took its name from the Second Earl of Dartmouth. In turn, his name was taken from the town that lies at the mouth of the River Dart in southern England. This street is one of a series of streets named for colleges or universities by the land developers of the Excelsior District, the University Homestead Association, in the 1860s.

DASHIELL HAMMETT Street: (formerly Monroe Street) In the 1920s Dashiell Hammett (1894–1961) lived on this street at Number 20, not far from where Miles Archer, Sam Spade's partner in Hammett's *The Maltese Falcon*, was killed by Brigid O'Shaughnessy.

DAVIDSON Avenue: Professor George Davidson was a surveyor. He helped to determine the boundaries between the United States and Canada as well as between Nevada and California. He became a professor of civil engineering at the University of California, Berkeley. Mount Davidson in San Francisco is named in his honor.

DAVIS Street: William Heath Davis, who was born in Honolulu, settled in California in 1838. A prominent merchant in San Francisco, Davis was also a shipowner and trader. Davis wrote a book called *Sixty Years in California*, one of the best treatises on San Francisco's pioneer days. The story goes that Davis raised only white cattle because "he could see them better."

DAWNVIEW Way: A good view of the dawn can be seen from this street on Twin Peaks. Incidentally, a parallel street is Sunview.

DEARBORN Street: Probably named for the Revolutionary War hero General Henry Dearborn. In 1803, as Secretary of War, he issued an order for a stockade and barracks to be built where Chicago now is, "with a view to the establishment of a Post." This became Fort Dearborn, later renamed Chicago.

DE BOOM Street: Cornelius De Boom was a pioneer and an early Belgian consul. De Boom was associated with Dr. John Townsend (who also has a street named for him) in the real-estate business.

DECATUR Street: Probably named after Stephen Decatur (1779–1820), a US. Naval officer whose ship, the *United States*, captured the British vessel Macedonian during the War of 1812. Decatur is credited with the expression, "Our country . . . may she always be right, but our country, right or wrong."

DECKER Alley: Peter W. Decker, born in Pennsylvania, arrived at Sutter's Fort, now Sacramento, via the Overland Route in 1849. Decker became mayor of Marysville in 1857, and two years later he established a bank there. Although his business interests were elsewhere, Decker purchased a residence in San Francisco, where he lived for a number of years before his death.

DE HARO Street: Francisco De Haro (1792–1848) was the first chief magistrate of Mexican Yerba Buena, the little village that became San Francisco. In 1839, he surveyed the area with the assistance of Captain Jean Jacques Vioget. After his twin sons were murdered by Americans under Kit Carson's command in 1846, he "declined and died of grief."

DELANCY Street: The two most southern blocks of First Street were renamed Delancy Street to recognize the contribution of the Delancy Street Foundation, a substance-abuse rehabilitation center, situated on these two blocks. The Delancy Street Foundation took its name from the street in New York City's lower East Side along which a great number of immigrants lived in the 19th Century. They adopted this name to symbolize a rebirth or new start which both the immigrants and foundation residents hoped to achieve. In turn, this street was named after James de Lancey, who became a New York Supreme Court judge in 1731 at the age of 28 and served as its Chief Justice from 1733 until he died in 1760.

DELMAR Street: In Spanish, this means "of the sea." It isn't an especially appropriate name for this street, since it is situated almost in the middle of the city.

DEL MONTE Street: This small street, which is located in the Outer Mission district, is not on a hill, however, the name in Spanish means "of the mountain."

DEL SUR Street: In Spanish this means "of the south." This street, however, is on the north side of Mt. Davidson.

DELLBROOK Avenue: This street runs from a group of eucalyptus trees, which might be considered a dell, to a dry creek bed, which may have once been a brook.

DELTA Place and Street: Delta is the fourth letter in the Greek alphabet. Alpha Street is nearby, but there is no Beta or Gamma Street.

DE SOTO Street: Ignacio De Soto was a soldier in Captain Juan Anza's expedition to San Francisco in 1776.

DETROIT Avenue: The city and river in Michigan are situated between Lake Erie and St. Clair Lake. The settlement there was founded on July 24, 1701, by a French trader, Antoine de la Mothe Cadillac. He named the fort Pontchartrain du Détroit, after his patron Comte de Pontchartrain, who was also Louis XIV's Minister of State. The British later simplified it to Detroit, which in French means "strait."

DEVONSHIRE Way: Devonshire is a district in southern England just east of Cornwall and former home of many emigrants to America. Some contractor or supervisor may have wanted to honor his ancestral home by so naming this street.

DEWEY Boulevard: Probably named for George Dewey (1837–1917), the US. naval commander whose men defeated the Spanish fleet at the Battle of Manila Bay during the Spanish-American War. Dewey was later promoted to admiral. The monument in the middle of Union Square was erected to honor Admiral Dewey.

DE WOLFE Street: William Morrison De Wolfe was a developer in the Richmond District of San Francisco at the turn of the 20th Century.

DIANA Street: She was the Roman goddess of the hunt. With strong associations as a fertility deity, she was called upon by women to aid in conception and delivery. Her name has the root *di* ("to shine") and probably means "bright one." A number of other streets in this part of San Francisco, Bayview, are also named for mythological gods and goddesses.

DIAZ Avenue: Possibly named after Manuel Díaz, a Mexican trader and shipmaster who came to California in 1843. He was serving as a magistrate in Monterey under Mexican rule. He was also a juror in the first jury trial ever held in California (1846). The street could also have been named for Brother Juan Díaz, a Franciscan, who accompanied Anza to San Gabriel and established a mission there.

DIVISADERO Street: Several explanations have been offered for the origin of the name of this street. The most reasonable version is that this is adapted from the Spanish word for "division," a very appropriate name for this street since it was once one dividing line between San Francisco and the Presidio. In 1906 the spelling of this street was changed from "divisidero" to "divisadero." Divisadero was once the western boundary of the City. It was first used to designate the western border of the City on an 1856 map of the area that was (and occasionally still is) known as the Western Addition. Another interpretation is that the word "divisadero" is derived from the Spanish *divisar* which means "to gaze from a distance." Nearby Lone Mountain was once called El Divisadero. This large hill is only about ten blocks west of this street. It is now part of the campus of the University of San Francisco. Additional credence is given to this interpretation by Zoeth S. Eldridge in *The Beginnings of San Francisco.* He wrote that the name comes from "divisadero: a point from which one can look far." Finally, some suggest that the word is derived from another Spanish word which means "summit of a great hill."

DIVISION Street: Named because it separates the North of Market area, where the streets run north/south and east/west, from the South of Market area, where the streets run northeast/southwest and northwest/southeast.

DIXIE Alley: This is the popular nickname of the southern states, especially those that belonged to the Confederacy (1860–65). According to the most common explanation, ten-dollar notes issued before 1860 by the Citizens' Bank of New Orleans and used primarily by Frenchspeaking residents, were imprinted with *Dix* (French for "ten") on the reverse side; hence the land of Dixies meant Louisiana and eventually was extended to refer to the whole South.

DOLORES Street: (Also Terrace) These streets were named for the mission and the mission church located alongside. But the official name of the Mission is San Francisco de Asis. A nearby lake that no longer exists was called *Laguna de la Nuestra Señora de Los Dolores,* "Lagoon of Our Lady of Sorrows." This is where the mission got its present name. This lake was named after the Virgin of Sorrows because the Spanish explorers discovered it on her feast day.

DOLPHIN Court: Named after the ocean mammal.

DONAHUE Street: Peter Donahue was called the "Father of California Industry." He established many enterprises: railroad lines that ran north and south from San Francisco; the Omnibus Street Railroad, the City's first streetcar line; and the San Francisco Gas Company, the first company of its kind in the West. The main source of Donahue's wealth, however, was the Union Iron Works, which he founded in 1849. This factory turned out stamp mills for mines in California and Nevada, the state's first printing press, the West's first heavy locomotive, and the Navy's first westcoast vessel, the *Saginaw,* as well as the warships *Comanche, Oregon,* and *Olympia.*

DONNER Avenue: George and Jacob Donner led a party of immigrants across a Sierra Nevada pass in winter of 1846–1847. Trapped in the High Sierra by early winter snows, some members resorted to anthropophagy, more commonly known as cannibalism.

DORADO Terrace: Dorado was one of the developers of the subdivision in Balboa Terrrace, where this street is located.

DORANTES Avenue: Dorantes was a member of Gaspar de Portolá's expedition to San Francisco in 1769.

DORCHESTER Way: Probably named after either the English town that is the county seat of Dorset, which was originally called Durnovaria in early Roman times, or else named after the large village in Oxfordshire, England, also called Dorchester, whose earlier names were Dorocina and Dorcic.

DORIC Alley: Probably named after the classic Greek column with a channeled shaft. The word also refers to a dialect, Doric, spoken by the Dorians, a linguistically distinct Greek people who conquered the Mycenaeans in the Peloponnesus.

DOW Place: William H. Dow was a leading merchant and shipping master in the 1850s. He was also one of the founders of the Howard Street Presbyterian Church.

DOWNEY Street: Possibly named after John G. Downey, Governor of California (1860–1862). Downey came to California as a Forty-Niner and worked in the gold mines near Grass Valley.

DOYLE Drive: Frank Pierce Doyle was a director of the Golden Gate Bridge Highway and Transportation District in the 1930s.

DRAKE Street: Probably named for Englishman Sir Francis Drake, circumnavigator of the world and the most renowned seaman of the Elizabethan period. In 1579, Drake anchored just north of San Francisco and took possession of the surrounding area, which he called Nova Albion. He was alleged to have left behind an inscribed plate. Such a plate originally attributed to Drake was discovered in the 1930s in Marin County. Later this plate was found to be a hoax.

DRUMM Street: Probably named for Lieutenant Richard Drum, an officer in the Mexican War of 1848 and later an adjutant general in the Pacific. Drum was stationed in San Francisco during the Civil War. There is only one "m," however, in the spelling of his name. Or the street may have been named after either John Drumm, who also served in the Civil War, or Andrew Drumm, a 49er gold prospector who spent about a year in San Francisco. After trying his luck in the mining areas, Drumm acquired a herd of cattle in Texas which he "drove" to the City. He apparently sold the animals for meat.

DUBLIN Street: The Irish capital's name originated from the fact that the city lies at the mouth of the River Liffey where it enters the Irish Sea. The dark bog water to be found here made the "black pool" which gave the town its name—*Dubh Linn* in Irish and *Dyfflin* in the language of the original Norse settlers. A number of streets in this part of town, the Crocker-Amazon district, were named for European capital cities.

DUBOCE Avenue: Colonel Victor D. Duboce commanded the first California regiment in the Spanish-American War of 1898.

DUKES Court: John and Sam Duke were attorneys who provided legal assistance to the community of Hunters Point during the 1960s when the Redevelopment Agency's project there was being built.

EAGLE Street: Possibly named for the sailing ship Eagle, which brought the first three Chinese persons to San Francisco in about 1846.

EARL Street: Forty-Niner John O. Earl was a member of the Vigilance Committee of 1851. Although it operated outside the law, this group of well-meaning citizens endeavored to impose their idea of order on the City's unruly elements. Earl later became a banker.

EASTWOOD Drive: All the streets in this Westwood Park subdivision end with the suffix "wood." This street is located on the east side of the tract.

ECKER Street: Pioneer George O. Ecker was a watchmaker and jeweler. In 1853 he became an assistant alderman of San Francisco.

EDDY Street: Probably named for William M. Eddy, a City surveyor in 1849. In 1851, Eddy made a new, enlarged map which extended streets laid out earlier by Jasper O'Farrell. In spite of his drinking, Eddy later became the State's surveyor general. Rodger Hotchin noted that, "given the fact that [Eddy] stayed drunk a goodly portion of his working day, it is a wonder that the [mapping] turned out as well as it did." Or possibly named for William H. Eddy, who survived the ill fated, trans-Sierra expedition of the Donner party in the winter of 1846–47 (although his wife, son, and daughter perished in the Sierra Nevada during the harsh winter).

EDGEHILL Way: This street is carved into the side of Edge Hill Mountain, its name derived from the fact that it is literally on the edge of a hill.

EDGEWOOD Avenue: The interior park belt—a forested open space near the campus of the University of California, San Francisco—is found at the south end of this street. However, one cannot see the woods for the plum trees.

EDINBURGH Street: The Scottish capital was named for the castle, built on a towering crag, around which the city was built. "Edin" comes from the Gaelic word *Eiden*, which may be derived from *Eden*, while *burgh* is the Scottish word for "borough."

EDITH Street: Possibly named after a pioneer.

EGBERT Avenue: Colonel Egbert was killed in the Philippines during the Spanish-American War.

EL CAMINO DEL MAR: Spanish for "the road of the sea," this is an appropriate name for a Sea Cliff thoroughfare which has a great view north towards the Golden Gate.

EL DORADO: Named after El Dorado County, California. This Spanish word means "golden" or "gilt." The Indians of Peru and other South American countries were constantly directing Spanish explorers to a land of fabulous wealth which was reputed to have a king whose body was covered every morning with gold dust. Thus the phrase "El Dorado" came to mean a region where gold and other precious metals were abundant.

ELGIN Park: Probably from the Scottish hymn "The Song of Elgin," based on the city of Elgin in Scotland. The "Park" was added by the developers to give more status to the street.

ELIZABETH Street: Probably named after a pioneer.

ELLERT Street: Levi Richard Ellert was the first mayor of San Francisco to be born in this City (October 20, 1857). In 1888 he was elected supervisor and in 1890 was reelected. Two years later, he was elected mayor. He owned a drug store when he began his political career, but during his mayoralty he studied law and became a lawyer.

ELLIS Street: Hotel owner Alfred J. Ellis came to California in 1847. He was a member of the State Constitutional Convention at Monterey in 1849, and a member of the San Francisco Board of Aldermen. Characterized as being "open handed and open hearted," he died in poverty.

ELLSWORTH Street: Possibly named after Elmer Ellsworth, a Civil War hero, who was famous for organizing the Chicago Zouaves and staging spectacular drill exhibitions throughout the country. After removing a Confederate flag from the roof of a the Marshal House Tavern in Alexandria, Virginia, on May 24, 1861, he was killed by the proprietor.

ELMIRA Street: (Also Drive) Probably named after the city in upstate New York. In 1828 Elmira, NY, was named for the daughter of an early settler, Nathan Teall.

EL MIRASOL: The Spanish word for "sunflower."

EL PLAZUELA: *Plazuela* means "small public square" in idiomatic Spanish.

EL POLIN Loop: The name is derived from the spring of the same name in the Presidio. The name "El Polin" is associated with a Spanish legend which said that all maidens who drank from this spring during the full moon were assured many children and eternal bliss. The spring was actively used by the early soldiers and settlers until 1846.

EL VERANO Way: The Spanish word for "summer." Why this word was selected as the name of this street remains unknown. What is known by most residents is that no book about San Francisco would be complete without the classic line attributed to Mark Twain: "The coldest winter I ever spent was a summer in San Francisco."

EMBARCADERO (The): The Spanish word for "point of embarkation" is an appropriate name for this waterfront street.

ENCANTO Avenue: The Spanish word for "charm" is an appropriate name for this attractive residential street.

ENCLINE Court: Perhaps named for the fact that this street is situated on a slight incline on the eastern slope of Mt. Davidson.

ENTRADA Court: This is Spanish for "entrance."

ERIE Street: Possibly named for the USS *Erie*, one of the military support ships in the Bay during the American take-over of San Francisco in 1846. This ship was named after the Indian tribe of Iroquoian linguistic stock who lived along the southern shore of Lake Erie from western New York to northern Ohio. Their name *erie, erike,* or *eriga* is usually interpreted as "long tail," in reference to panthers. This is why the tribe is called the Cat Nation.

ESCONDIDO Avenue: This Spanish word for "hidden" is an appropriate name for this street because it is secluded in the area near Pine Lake Park in the southwest part of the City.

ESMERALDA Avenue: This Spanish word means "emerald."

ESPANOLA Street: Espanola Jackson was a prominent community leader in Hunters Point during the Redevelopment Agency's project there in the 1960s.

ESQUINA Drive: This Spanish word means "corner."

ESSEX Street: The USS *Essex* was a famous warship which was commanded by Commodore David Porter in the War of 1812.

ESTERO Avenue: This Spanish word translates as "estuary," but it is also used to mean "an inlet" or "lagoon near the sea."

EUCLID Avenue: Possibly named after the street in Cleveland, Ohio, which was named for Euclid, the most prominent of the ancient Greek mathematicians. Euclid was best known for his treatise on geometry, *The Elements.* Since surveyors and cartographers make extensive use of his contributions, it is little wonder that Euclid's name is often selected as a street name.

EUGENIA Avenue: Popular legend has it that Eugenia was the beautiful daughter of the toll keeper on San Bruno Road before the turn of the 20th Century.

EUREKA Street: This word is Greek for "I have found it." It was the famous exclamation of Archimedes, a well-known ancient Greek mathematician and philosopher, after he had solved the problem of distinguishing between pure gold and gold alloyed with silver by observing the relative water displacement of both substances. The word was adopted in 1850 as California's motto and is included in the state seal.

EVANS Avenue: Rear Admiral Robley D. Evans led vessels from the great white fleet of the United States Navy on a world tour in 1907. President Theodore Roosevelt dispatched these ships to "show the flag" and display America's military power. Their arrival in San Francisco harbor produced a large burst of social activities.

EWER Place: Possibly named for Ferdinand Ewer, a pioneer journalist and minister.

EXCELSIOR Avenue: This word means "more lofty," "more elevated," or "higher" in Greek and is an appropriate name for a street leading to the hills of McLaren Park.

EXECUTIVE PARK Boulevard: Named for the office park in which this road is situated.

EXETER Street: Probably named after the cathedral city situated on the River Exe in southwest England.

FAIR Avenue: James G. Fair was born in Dublin in 1831. He first worked in California as a pick-and-shovel miner. A rival of the Comstock kings, William C. Ralston and William Sharon, Fair eventually became a US Senator. In the City's first act of redevelopment, "Bonanza Jim" acquired ownership of the land on which the Fairmont Hotel is now situated. He intended to build a grand mansion for his family, but his marriage broke up before he was able to construct the house.

FAIRFAX Avenue: Probably named for Charles ("Lord") Fairfax, originally of Fairfax County, Virginia, who settled in Marin County in 1856.

FAIRMOUNT Street: This street once led directly to Fairmount Plaza (now Fairmount Park), and both the street and the park are located in what was once the Fairmont Tract.

FAITH Street: The street next to this one is named Joy. This street was named for a basic human belief. It is also possible that it was the name of a pioneer.

FALLON Place: A Canadian, Thomas Fallon arrived in California in 1844 and took an active part in the Bear Flag Revolt two years later. Fallon was the first to raise the United States flag in San Jose. He went on to become a successful placer miner and San Francisco businessman.

FALMOUTH Street: Probably named after the town in Cornwall, England, which received its name because it is located near the mouth of the River Fal.

FANNING Way: A well-known engineer, Charles Fanning worked for the City's Real Estate Department. He was in charge of the property transactions for the Golden Gate Heights project that was carried out in the late 1920s by Michael M. O'Shaughnessy, San Francisco's chief engineer.

FARALLONES Street: (Farallon, singular) Spanish for "headlands" or "high rocks which stand out in the sea." Even though the seven islands are about 32 miles out to sea, they are within San Francisco's City boundary.

FARRAGUT Avenue: At the age of 11, David Glasgow Farragut (later an admiral) fought in the War of 1812. In the 1840s, Farragut was sent to California from Washington D.C. to establish the Mare Island Navy Yard near Vallejo.

FARVIEW Court: One of a series of streets in the Midtown Terrace subdivision with the suffix "view." The name rings true, since this street is on the slopes of Twin Peaks and has a good view.

FAXON Avenue: Probably named for Faxon Dean Atherton, a landowner in San Mateo County.

FEDERAL Street: Probably named for the US bonded federal warehouse once located nearby.

FELL Street: Born in Denmark, merchant William C. Fell arrived in San Francisco in 1849. He was a member of the Society of California Pioneers.

FELTON Street: Charles Norton Felton (1832–1914) came to California during the Gold Rush and went into the pickle business. He made his fortune, however, by investing in the mines of the Nevada Comstock Lode. Later, he developed the Snow Mountain Water and Power Company in Lake and Mendocino counties. He served as an assemblyman and a US congressman, and he replaced US Senator George Hearst after Hearst's death.

FERNWOOD Drive: Named after members of the plant family. One of a series of streets in Westwood Highlands that have the same suffix.

FILLMORE Street: Millard Fillmore (1800–1874) was the thirteenth President of the United States, from 1850 to 1853. A moderate Whig politician, he insisted on federal enforcement of the Fugitive Slave Act of 1850, which alienated the North and led to the demise of the Whig party.

FITCH Street: George K. Fitch was a wellknown pioneer and newspaperman. He was co-owner of the *Alta California*, the *Call*, and the *Bulletin* (which he also edited from 1856 to 1897). Under Fitch, the *Bulletin* waged a war for economy in municipal financing and decried the domination of the Republican and Democratic parties by the Southern Pacific Railroad.

FLINT Street: Named for Addison R. Flint.

FLOOD Avenue: Flood arrived in California during the Gold Rush and he, James Fair, John MacKay and William S. O'Brien became known as the Bonanza Kings, as they all made their fortunes mining silver in Nevada.

FLORA Street: Probably named after the Roman goddess of budding springtime, fruit trees, vines, and flowers. It might also have been the name of a pioneer.

FLORENCE Street: Possibly named after the Italian city which was originally called Florentina—"the flourishing town." This street may also have been named for a pioneer.

FLORENTINE Avenue: (see above)

FLORIDA Street: The state was named after the Spanish word for "flowery." The area was named by Ponce de Leon, who discovered it on Easter Sunday (*Pascua Florida*) in 1512.

FOLSOM Street: Colonel Jonathan Stevenson led a group of New York volunteers who fought in the Mexican War. In 1847 many of these soldiers arrived in Yerba Buena Harbor by boat. One of these individuals was Captain Joseph L. Folsom. Folsom made and then lost a fortune in real estate. He was notorious for hiring thugs to force squatters off his property. He founded the town bearing his name on the American River, carving it out of a large land grant that he acquired from the Liedesdorff family. He and millionaire Sam Brannan were among a long list of landed men who paid no taxes—the City government was not yet powerful enough in 1855 to face down its barons.

FONT Boulevard: Father Pedro Font was a chaplain with Captain Juan Anza's party on its journey from Mexico to San Francisco in 1776. His diary entry on March 27, 1776, reads "The port of San Francisco is a wonder of nature, and may be called the port of ports, on account of its great capacity and the various heights included in its littoral or shore and in its islands."

FOREST KNOLLS Drive: This road rims the Forest Knolls subdivision situated on the slope of Mt. Sutro.

FOREST SIDE Avenue: Situated on the side of a nameless hill where an abundance of eucalyptus, pine, bottlebrush, and palm trees line the sidewalk. Although it is not a forest, the vegetation does produce a sylvan setting. This street also marks the edge of Sutro Forest.

FOREST VIEW Drive: This road ends (or begins) at Eucalyptus Drive. At the present time, however, one can find neither eucalyptus trees nor a forest in the vicinity, but Stern Grove and Pine Lake Park are not far away and may have been the inspiration for these names.

FORTUNA Avenue: In Roman mythology, Fortuna was the goddess of good fortune.

FRANCE Avenue: The country's name was derived from the Franks, who occupied the area in the Middle Ages.

FRANCISCO Street: Probably named after St. Francis of Assisi, for whom this city was named. (See the Bay Area Landmarks section of this book for a more detailed discussion.)

FRANCONIA Street: There once was a roadhouse with this name on the old toll road that is now San Bruno Avenue. In turn, the roadhouse was named for an area that is now part of Germany. Originally inhabited by the Franks who settled there in the Sixth Century A.D., it includes Bavaria, Baden-Württemberg, Hessen, East Franconia, and Rhineland-Pfalz.

FRANK NORRIS Street: (formerly the eastern half of Austin Street) Born in Chicago, novelist Frank Norris (1870–1902) moved to San Francisco in 1884. He grew up on Sacramento Street, near Polk Street, which is the site of his greatest book, *McTeague*. Both his joyous *Blix* and his gritty, realistic *McTeague* were published in 1889, and each exemplifies a curious bridge between frontier romanticism and a new muscular realism.

FRANKLIN Street: This street may have been named for either Selim Franklin, a pioneer merchant, or Benjamin Franklin (1706–1790), the noted printer, publisher, author, inventor, scientist, and diplomat who helped write both the Declaration of Independence and the US Constitution.

FREELON Street: An active magistrate and county judge of the court of sessions, T. W. Freelon administered the oath of office to Mayor S. P. Webb in 1854.

FREEMAN Court: Brigadier General Henry B. Freeman was commanding officer of the Presidio for twenty days in April 1899. He received the Medal of Honor for saving a wounded fellow officer under fire during the Civil War.

FREMONT Street: General John Charles Frémont (the son of a Frenchman—hence the accent mark) took an active part in the Bear Flag Revolt and the conquest of California. His political career was varied. In early 1847 Frémont was briefly the civil and military governor of the state, in 1850–1851, a US Senator from California, and an unsuccessful candidate for president in 1856. Although a Southerner by birth, Frémont remained in the Union Army during the Civil War because he was opposed to the secession.

FRESNO Street: *Fresno* is Spanish for the ash tree, which is found in abundance in the southern part of California's Central Valley, where this city is located.

FRIENDSHIP Court: This thoroughfare is situated in Friendship Village, part of the Western Addition AII Redevelopment Project. The name was selected for the sponsors of the project: The First Friendship Institute Baptist Church.

FRONT Street: At one time, this street was located on the shoreline, but since part of the Bay has been filled in, it is now several blocks from the waterfront.

FUENTE Avenue: Pedro Perez de Fuente was an early settler.

FULTON Street: Possibly named after either an early pioneer, Daniel J., or the inventor of the steamboat, Robert.

FUNSTON Avenue: Named in 1923 to honor Brigadier General Frederick Funston, acting commander of the Army's Pacific Division during the difficult days after the 1906 earthquake and fire. Funston's forces were in charge of maintaining law and order in the devastated streets. Two streets named for this general are found in San Francisco: one in the Presidio, and the other in the Richmond District between 12th and 14th avenues. It would be 13th Avenue if it were not for the superstitions associated with that number.

GABILAN Way: The Spanish word for "sparrow hawk." There are several other streets with Spanish names in this part of the Outer Sunset district which abuts Pine Lake Park.

GALILEE Lane: This is a fitting name for a street in St. Francis Square, a housing project sponsored by the International Longshoremen's Union. The *Galilee* was a two-masted brigantine that sailed the South Seas.

GALINDO Avenue: Jose Galindo owned 2,200 acres of land within what are now the City's limits during the Mexican control of San Francisco.

GALVEZ Avenue: José Gálvez, Visitador-General of Spain and a member of the Council of the Indies in Mexico City, organized, equipped, and dispatched an expedition commanded by Gaspar de Portolá in 1769, which went from San Diego to San Francisco.

GARCES Drive: Brother Francisco Garcés, a Franciscan religious official, accompanied Captain Juan Anza to San Gabriel, a mission town several miles east of present-day Los Angeles. In 1791 Garcés and Captain Rivera y Moncada were en route to California with a group via the Sonora Trail in northern Mexico when they were ambushed by Yuma Indians, and everyone in the party was killed. (See also Moncada Way.)

GARCIA Avenue: Garcia is a common Spanish surname.

GARDEN Street: This block-long alley may have been the site of a garden at one time, but now only a few homes and parking lots are found here.

GARDENSIDE Drive: Situated on the side of Twin Peaks, this street may have been the location of a garden in former years, but now only small apartment buildings are found on either side of this street.

GARLINGTON Court: Ethel Garlington was a well-known community leader during the 1960s at Hunters Point when the Redevelopment Agency's project there was being developed.

GARRISON Avenue: Only six months after his arrival, Cornelius K. Garrison became San Francisco's fourth mayor, on October 1, 1853. Born near West Point, New York, Garrison was a shipbuilder on the Great Lakes before moving to San Francisco during the Gold Rush.

GATES Street: Horatio Gates (1728–1806) was a general during the Revolutionary War. His decisive defeat of the British at the Battle of Saratoga in 1777 turned the tide for the colonists.

GATEVIEW Court: This street affords a view of the Golden Gate, hence the name.

GAVEN Street: Gaven was a surveyor and draftsman employed by the Crocker Banking and Land Company. He helped lay out the Crocker estate in the Silver Terrace district, where this street is located, and probably named the road after himself.

GAVIOTA Way: Spanish for "seagull."

GEARY Street: (Also Expressway and Boulevard) John White Geary was San Francisco's last *alcalde* and first mayor (elected under the new city charter in 1850). In recognition of services rendered during the Mexican War, President Polk appointed Geary San Francisco's first postmaster. Geary gave the City the land now known as Union Square. After leaving the City, Geary became a general in the Union Army during the Civil War. Later, Geary had the unusual distinction of being elected governor of Kansas and subsequently, governor of Pennsylvania.

GELLERT Drive: Probably named for a contractor who may have built homes in this southwestern part of San Francisco near Lake Merced.

GENEBERN Way: Brother Genebern was one of the original faculty members of St. Mary's College which was located where this street is today from 1863 until 1899.

GENESSEE Street: Probably named for the region in Upstate New York. The word is originally an Indian one which means "beautiful valley" in the Iroquoian language.

GENEVA Avenue: The city in upstate New York was named after the wellknown city and lake in Switzerland. The original name of Geneva (or Genava) dates back to the pre-Celtic Ligurian peoples. This is but one of a series of streets named for upstate New York cities in the south-central part of San Francisco. Niagara and Seneca avenues, for example, are nearby.

GENOA Place: The name of Genoa (or Genova), a major Italian port city, is derived from the pre-Celtic Ligurian people.

GEORGE Court: George Williams was a prominent community leader in Hunters Point during the 1960s when the Redevelopment Agency's project was being built.

GERKE Alley: Henry Gerke arrived in San Francisco in July 1846, and was an original member of the board of directors of the Society of California Pioneers. Since Gerke was a successful wholesaler of California wines and brandies, he was one of the largest taxpayers in San Francisco, paying $755 in 1850.

GERMANIA Street: As early as 1855, a community of five to six thousand German families were located in the section of San Francisco known as

Duboce Park. This street, located at the foot of the park, was named after their native country. Franklin Hospital, which is situated in this area, was once called German Hospital.

GIANTS Drive: This street, situated within sight of Candlestick Park, was named after San Francisco's baseball team. It may well be the only street in America carrying the name of a National (or, for that matter, American) League baseball club.

GIBSON Road: Brigadier General Horatio G. Gibson was post commander of the Presidio in 1856 and on two different occasions in 1859. When he died in 1924 at the age of 94, Gibson was the oldest living graduate of West Point.

GILBERT Street: In 1847 Lieutenant Edward Gilbert was a member of Stevenson's Regiment, a group of soldiers from New York who came to California for adventure and to liberate, if necessary, California from Mexican control. A printer by trade, Gilbert was editor of the *Alta California* and later, a California congressman. He was killed in a duel at the age of 30.

GILMAN Avenue: Daniel Coit Gilman was an American reformer of higher education. As president of the University of California, Gilman advocated giving less attention to classical subjects.

GILROY Street: Probably named for John Gilroy, the first permanent, non-Spanish settler in California. In 1814, this Scottish sailor either deserted or was put ashore at Monterey because of scurvy. His real name was Cameron but, being a minor, he adopted his mother's maiden name for fear of deportation.

GLADEVIEW Way: One of a series of streets with the suffix "view" in the Midtown Terrace subdivision on the west slope of Twin Peaks.

GLENBROOK Avenue: *Glenn* is a Celtic word meaning "narrow valley." It was an obsolete geographical name that was revived by the romantic movement in the 19th Century.

GLENVIEW Drive: A view of Glen Park may be seen from this road. One of a series of streets with the suffix "view" in the Midtown Terrace subdivision on the south slope of Twin Peaks.

GOETHE Street: Johann Wolfgang von Goethe (1749–1832), a German, is a giant of world literature. Although he was a critic, a journalist, a painter, a theater manager, a statesman, a novelist, an educator, a playwright, a poet, a scientist, and a natural philosopher, Goethe is best known for his drama "Faust."

GOETTINGEN Street: Probably named after the town in Germany.

GOLD Street: Reputedly the City's first assay office was situated on this alley. Here those lucky few who struck pay dirt could bring their treasure to be weighed and exchanged for cash.

GOLD MINE Drive: Named for Gold Mine Hill, around which this street winds. It was named by the Redevelopment Agency in the mid-Sixties.

GOLDEN GATE Avenue: Originally called Tyler Street for John Tyler, tenth President of the United States, the street became Golden Gate Park's driveway in 1880 when the Park opened. General John Charles Frémont first coined the expression "Golden Gate." (For more on this subject see the section on Bay Area Landmarks in this book.)

GOLETA Avenue: This is the Spanish word for "schooner." There are several other Spanish names on parallel streets in this subdivision adjacent to Pine Lake Park.

GONZALEZ Drive: José Manuel Gonzalez, born in Sonora, Mexico, brought his wife and four children to San Francisco in 1776 with Captain Juan Anza's party.

GORDON Street: George C. Gordon was an Englishman who, in the early 1850s, developed South Park as a select residential area for wealthy families. He also helped establish the City's first immigration society in 1855. It was committed to making the Bay Area a more attractive destination for immigrants by lowering overland and ship fares, encouraging vigilance groups, and hastening the completion of a transcontinental railroad.

GOUGH Street: Charles H. Gough, a busy milkman, rode through San Francisco on horseback with a milk can on either side of his saddle in the 1850s. By 1855, Gough had been appointed to a committee to name the streets of the Western Addition, so he named one for himself and one for his sister. (See Octavia Street.)

GRACE Street: A relative or friend of a pioneer.

GRANADA Avenue: Probably named for the city and province in southern Spain. The name may have been derived from either the Spanish for "pomegranate," fruit that appears on Granada's coat of arms, or from its Moorish name, *Kamattah* (*Garnatah*) which possibly means "hill of strangers."

GRAND VIEW Avenue: (also Terrace) A street near Upper Market that lives up to its name—a splendid view of the City is available along its way. The geographical center of the City (land only) lies between 23rd and Alvarado streets on the east side of Grand View Avenue.

GRANT Avenue: Ulysses S. Grant was the commanding general of the Union Army for part of the Civil War and later the eighteenth President of the United States. In 1876, the section of this street from Bush to Market was changed from Du Pont Street to Grant Avenue. In 1908, the rest of Du Pont Street became Grant Avenue. Du Pont Street had been named for Captain Samuel F. Du Pont, a naval officer on the *Conquest* and a friend of Washington Bartlett, for whom a street is also named. Grant Avenue is considered to be the oldest street in the City—it was originally called Calle de la Fundación. The first building in San Francisco, a semipermanent tent, was erected by William Richardson on June 25, 1835, at what is now 827 Grant Avenue.

GREAT Highway: In 1874 the California legislature named this road, which parallels the Pacific Ocean on the City's western edge. Today it is still a "great highway" which has two lanes of traffic going in each direction; separated part of the way by parking areas.

GREEN Street: Talbot H. Green was a leading San Francisco merchant who acquired considerable property and wealth in the ten years prior to 1851. In a letter, Green once wrote: "The traders [here] are a sharp set, dog eat dog." While a candidate for mayor, Green was identified as Paul Geddes, an embezzler who had left his wife and children in the East. Immediately, Green left for the East, claiming he could disprove the charge. He never did. He was, however, taken back by his wife and family, and he repaid the money he owed.

GREENVIEW Court: One of a series of streets with the suffix "view" off of Panorama Drive in the Midtown Terrace subdivision on the northwest slope of Twin Peaks.

GREENWICH Street: (also Terrace) Named by Jean Jacques Vioget after a street with the same name in New York City. Vioget, a Swiss sailor and surveyor, laid out many of San Francisco's streets in 1839. The street in New York was probably named after Greenwich, England, through which the standard time meridian passes. It is also the home of the British Naval Academy.

GREENWOOD Avenue: One of a series of streets in the Westwood Park subdivision with the same suffix—"wood."

GRIFFITH Street: Pioneer Millen Griffith arrived in San Francisco in 1849. Capitalizing on the needs of the harbor, he operated a small hauling business, which soon expanded into a fleet of tug boats. In addition, Griffith was a partner in the Pacific Steam Whaling Company.

GRIJALVA Drive: Sergeant Juan Pablo Grijalva was born in 1742 in Sonora, Mexico. A member of Captain Juan Anza's party, Grijalva brought with him his wife and three children.

GROVE Street: Although there is no orchard or grove on this street now, it is possible that this street was named after a grove of trees or some other comparable vegetation.

GUERRERO Street: Francisco Guerrero was a highly respected Mexican citizen who held local offices before and after the American occupation of 1846. Guerrero had extensive land holdings near Half Moon Bay. In 1851, he was murdered when he was struck in the back of the head by a projectile from a slingshot. Guerrero was a witness in a celebrated murder trail, and it was presumed that he was killed to silence his testimony.

HAHN Street: John Hahn was president of the Visitacion Valley Homestead Association as well as a property owner in that neighborhood in the late 1860s. This street is located in Visitation Valley.

HAIGHT Street: There are three versions of the origin of this street name. The most likely possibility is that it is named after Henry Haight, a City supervisor and a manager of the early banking firm of Page, Bacon and Company. Haight was instrumental in the founding of the Protestant Orphanage, since he gave the land for it. A less likely namesake is Fletcher M. Haight, Henry's brother, who was a prominent lawyer and later a United States district judge. The third and least likely prospect is H. H. Haight, an early California governor.

HALE Street: John Hale was a leader in the Irish community of the Outer Mission. He was employed by the Crocker Land and Banking Company, which at one time owned the land where the street is located.

HALLECK Street: A lawyer, an army officer and an expert on fortifications, Major General Henry W. Halleck was appointed the secretary of state of California in 1847. He is reputed to have drafted parts of the California Constitution. Halleck also served as general-in-chief of the Union Army from 1862 to 1864. Halleck funded the construction of the Montgomery Block, which was destroyed to make way for the Transamerica Building, the tallest building in San Francisco. Two "Halleck" streets are found in San Francisco—one in the downtown financial district, the other in the Presidio.

HAMILTON Street: Named after the college and town in upstate New York, which was named for Alexander Hamilton, the first US Secretary of the Treasury and an advocate of a strong central government for the former colonies. Hamilton was the primary author of *The Federalist Papers*. He was mortally wounded in a duel with Aaron Burr.

HAMPSHIRE Street: Probably named after New Hampshire, which, in turn, was named for the district in south-central England. Both this and the adjacent street, York, which is also named for an English geographical area, were probably the sites of homes of early settlers.

HANCOCK Street: Possibly named after John Hancock (1737–1793), a leader in the American Revolution and, as president of the Continental Congress, the first person to sign the Declaration of Independence.

HANOVER Street: Probably named after the district and city (Hannover) in western Germany which may have been the birthplace of a pioneer.

HARDIE Street: Major General James A. Hardie was the first commanding officer of the Presidio under the United States flag.

HARDING Road: This road leads to the Harding Park golf course. Both the park and the road were named for Warren G. Harding, twenty-ninth President of the United States (1921–23). Harding died unexpectedly in San Francisco's Palace Hotel during his third year in office. His term is remembered as one of widespread corruption.

HARE Street: Named for Elias C. Hare, about whom not much is known.

HARLAN Place: Accompanied by his wife and four children, George W. Harlan led an overland party to California in 1846. He soon enlisted in the US Army and fought in the Mexican War. After his discharge, he and his family purchased a ranch between San Jose and San Francisco; they were then the only Americans living between these two communities.

HARNEY Way: Charles L. Harney was an important San Francisco builder in the mid-20th Century. Candlestick Park was one of his projects.

HARRIET Street: Named for a daughter of Immanuel Charles Christian Russ. He owned Russ Gardens, the amusement park that was once located nearby.

HARRIS Place: Probably named for Stephen R. Harris, mayor of San Francisco in 1852. Harris was a physician who came to California in June 1849. He was the fourth president of the Society of California Pioneers. After his term, Harris served as controller, then coroner of the City.

HARRISON Street: Probably named for Edward H. Harrison, who became a port collector and a member of the Town Council shortly after arriving in San Francisco in 1847. Subsequently, he became a prominent merchant. A less likely namesake is William Henry Harrison, the ninth President of the United States and the first to die in office (1841).

HARTFORD Street: The capital city of Connecticut was named after the English town, Hertford. The spelling difference may have been due to the pronunciation of the English name.

HARVARD Street: The university in Cambridge, Massachusetts was named for John Harvard, a Puritan minister who left his books and half his estate to the educational institution in the 1630s.

HAWES Street: Horace Hawes was a prominent lawyer during the Gold Rush and was the chief executive officer of the City under the first mayor, John W. Geary. Hawes later served in the State Assembly and Senate, where he introduced a bill consolidating the City and County of San Francisco, the only joint city-county in California.

HAWTHORNE Street: Probably named after a ship that brought pioneers to California.

HAYES Street: Colonel Thomas Hayes was the San Francisco county clerk from 1853 to 1856. His brother Michael was one of the three members of the committee that named the streets in the Western Addition and was probably responsible for this street name. Hayes was also the developer of Hayes Valley, a residential neighborhood west of the Civic Center.

HEARST Avenue: George Hearst was born in 1820 in Franklin County, Missouri. A Forty-Niner, he struck it rich in Virginia City, Nevada, with the Comstock Lode, an especially rich vein of silver. Hearst purchased the *San Francisco Examiner,* which his son William Randolph used as the flagship of his vast commercial empire that consisted of newspapers, radio stations, movie studios, and publishing houses. George Hearst was appointed a US Senator in 1886 and served in this position until 1891.

HELENA Street: Named either for a woman named Helena, or for the capital of Montana, which was also named for a woman.

HENRY ADAMS Street: Henry Adams was a realtor who developed both the Showplace Square and the Galleria, two wholesale trade centers located on this thoroughfare. These two blocks were formerly the beginning of Kansas Street, but after Adams died of a heart attack in 1981, this part of the street was renamed in his honor.

HERBST Road: (formerly Zoo Road) Named for Herman and his brother, Maurice Herbst. Originally the owners of a sheet metal shop, they bought San Francisco real estate, particularly office and business properties on Market and Mission streets. They established a foundation that helped to pay for the renovation of the theatre that bears their name in the Veterans Building, the auditorium at Mt. Zion Hospital, and the pool and gymnasium at the Recreation Center for the Handicapped. They died within three months of each other in 1967. Formerly Zoo Road, this street leads to a south gate entrance to the zoo, which is another beneficiary of the Herbst Foundation.

HERMANN Street: Sigismund Hermann (1816–1890) was born in Mecklenburg, Germany, and arrived in San Francisco in 1849. One year later, Hermann opened a dry goods and general merchandise business which lasted for two decades. In addition to being a successful merchant, Hermann was briefly an insurance agent, a member of the Board of Trade, a real-estate investor, and a hops trader.

HERNANDEZ Avenue: Hernandez is a common Spanish surname.

HERON Street: Ensign James H. Heron was born in Richmond, Virginia, in 1827. Heron first arrived in California in 1846 on the USS *Levant.* After fighting in the Mexican War, he returned to California in 1862. Starting out as a messenger, Heron worked for Wells Fargo and Company for 26 years. His final position with the company was that of secretary.

HIDALGO Terrace: In the early Middle Ages, this was a Spanish term denoting hereditary nobles and knights. Later, it became a common Spanish surname.

HIGH Street: At approximately 600-feet high and one block in length, this street is certainly the highest short or shortest high street in San Francisco.

HIGUERA Avenue: Born in 1753 in Sinaloa, Mexico, Ygnasio Anastasio Higuera came with his 13-year-old wife to San Francisco in 1776 with Captain Juan Anza's party. Two years later, their son was baptized at Mission Dolores.

HILL Street: (and Drive) Appropriately named for a street that goes up and down a steep incline on the eastern slope of Twin Peaks.

HILL CREST Court: An appropriate name for this little street located almost atop the City's highest peak—Mt. Davidson.

HILL POINT Avenue: This street climbs up (or down) the hill towards the top (or bottom) of Mt. Sutro.

HILLWAY Avenue: This street, parallel to Hill Point, also ascends and descends Mt. Sutro.

HINCKLEY Walk: William S. Hinckley arrived in San Francisco in 1830. A city official in 1844, Hinckley later became captain of the port and eventually, mayor of San Francisco.

HOFFMAN Street: Brigadier General William Hoffman was the commanding officer of the Presidio for a brief period in 1859.

HOLLAND Court: Democrat Nathaniel Holland was an assistant alderman in 1851. Three years later, he was elected to the State Assembly.

HOLLISTER Avenue: Sergeant Stanley Hollister of California was killed in Cuba during the Spanish-American War.

HOLLOWAY Avenue: Possibly named after William Holloway who came from New York City in 1883. He died from a horseback fall eleven years later. During Holloway's career he was the United States consul in Peru and Uruguay.

HOLLY PARK Circle: An appropriately named street, since it completely circumscribes Holly Park.

HOLLYWOOD Court: This street is situated in a subdivision that was marketed as, and is still known locally as, Little Hollywood. It is doubtful, however, if even one starlet ever lived here.

HOLYOKE Street: Named after the Massachusetts college that was named for the explorer, Elizor Holyoke. This is one of a series of streets in the Excelsior district that were named for colleges or universities in the 1860s by the developers, the University Homestead Association.

HOMER Street: Probably named after the Greek poet and author of the *Iliad* and the *Odyssey*, the two greatest epic poems of ancient Greece. Scholars believe he was an Ionian who lived in either the eighth or the ninth Century B.C.

HOMEWOOD Court: (also Terrace) One of a series of streets in Westwood Park that have the same suffix.

HOPKINS Avenue: Probably named in honor of Mark Hopkins (1813–1878). In 1849 Hopkins came to Sacramento, California and became a partner with Collis P. Huntington in a general merchandise store. This association led to Hopkins becoming one of the "Big Four"—the builders of the Central Pacific Railroad. His principal duties were to supervise and control the finances of the railroad and its many affiliated companies.

HORACE Street: The famous ancient Roman lyric poet and satirist's most frequent themes were love, friendship, philosophy, and the art of poetry. This street is only one block away from a street named for another Latin poet, Virgil.

HOTALING Street: Anson Parsons Hotaling was born in New Baltimore, New York. While still a young man, Hotaling sailed around Cape Horn, arriving in California in 1852. After working briefly in the placer mines, Hotaling made his fortune operating a wholesale liquor business. He also owned real estate in San Francisco, Marin, and San Mateo counties and founded a savings bank in San Rafael.

HOUSTON Street: The Texas city was named for Samuel B. Houston, the first and third president of the Republic of Texas (1836–38; 1841–44). In 1836, two New York land speculators bought a site near the burned-out village of Harrisburg, Texas. Two months after this purchase, one of them proposed that the first congress of the Republic of Texas, then in session at Columbia, move the government to his town. After much persuasion, the congress agreed. The government, however, stayed only two years before the maneuver was denounced as corrupt. After Texas joined the Union in 1845, Samuel Houston became a US Senator.

HOWARD Street: William Davis Merry Howard was one of the City's most publicspirited and prosperous men. A merchant, Howard was known as the first citizen of San Francisco in the period just before the Gold Rush. In 1847, he was elected to San Francisco's first city council. Four years later, Howard was one of fourteen persons who organized the first Vigilance committee and, subsequently, the City's first fire company.

HUDSON Avenue: While trying to find a shorter route from Europe to Asia, the English navigator Henry Hudson discovered the Hudson River and Hudson's Bay.

HUGO Street: Victor Hugo (1802–1885), a French poet, dramatist, and novelist, was an important French romantic writer. In later life, Hugo used his great power to shape French public opinion. He is known for his novels *The Hunchback of Notre Dame* and *Les Miserables*. A street one block away is named for another author, Washington Irving.

HUMBOLDT Street: Baron Alexander von Humboldt (1769–1859) was a famous German natural philosopher, scientist, and explorer. He journeyed to the upper regions of the Amazon and Orinoco rivers in South America. In *Cosmos*, one of the world's great scientific works, he sought to formulate the known facts about the universe into a uniform conception of nature.

HUNT Street: Henry Brown Hunt (1836–1893) was a pioneer merchant. A native of New Jersey, Hunt arrived in San Francisco in 1849. He held a variety of jobs in the gold country and Sacramento before forming a wholesale liquor firm in San Francisco in 1880.

HUNTERS POINT Boulevard: (also Expressway) This street is named for the area through which it goes. In turn, the area received its name from one of two possible sources. In 1849, Robert E. Hunter and his brother, Philip participated in the development of a new city which was to be called South San Francisco. Alternatively, this area may be called Hunters Point because sportsmen from San Francisco went hunting there.

HUNTINGTON Drive: Collis P. Huntington came west with the Forty-Niners. Trading with miners, he became a merchant and operated a store in Sacramento. Huntington was one of the "Big Four" along with Charles Crocker, Leland Stanford, and Mark Hopkins. They built the Central Pacific, the first railroad to connect California with major cities in the east.

HURON Avenue: These Iroquois-speaking, North American Indians, lived along the St. Lawrence River when it was discovered by the French explorer, Jacques Cartier in 1534.

HYDE Street: George Hyde arrived in California in 1846. About a year later, Hyde was appointed *alcalde* (mayor) of San Francisco following Bartlett and Bryant (for whom streets were also named). Hyde had been Commodore Stockton's secretary. (See Stockton Street.)

ICEHOUSE Alley: Formerly Gaines Street, this thoroughfare was named for the two ice houses situated on either side of it—the buildings now contain offices.

IGNACIO Avenue: A common Spanish surname.

ILLINOIS Street: The state was named for the Indian tribe who called themselves the *Inini*, "perfect and accomplished men." The French called them *Illini* and added the suffix *-ois* to denote the tribe. In the mid-17th Century there were 6,500 such Indians living in what is now southern Wisconsin, northern Illinois and parts of Iowa and Missouri, but by 1800 only 150 of them remained.

INCA Lane: The *Inca*, built in 1896, was a five-masted schooner, the second of her rig on the Pacific Coast. On October 10, 1920, she left Eureka bound for Sydney with a cargo of redwood lumber. On December 7th, she was dismasted in a storm and abandoned by all but two of her crew. Eleven days later, she was found and towed into Sydney harbor, where she was sold for scrap. With such a dishonorable end to her maritime career, it is curious that a street in her honor is named in a housing project sponsored by the International Longshoremen's Union.

INDIANA Street: The state's name was derived from the Latin form of *Indian* meaning "land of the Indians." Originally, the word referred to that portion of land which was carved out of the Northwest Territory in 1800 to become the territory and later the state of Indiana.

INDUSTRIAL Street: This street is located in an industrial area.

INFANTRY Terrace: Named in 1923 after this branch of the Army. It is an appropriate name for a street in the Presidio.

INGALLS Street: General Rufus Ingalls was an early landowner in Benicia.

INGERSON Avenue: Doctor H. H. Ingerson was an early citizen of San Francisco.

INNES Avenue: George Innes (1825–1894) was an American painter noted for the luminous quality of his later landscapes.

INVERNESS Drive: The town in west Marin County was probably named for the county and town of the same name in Scotland. The street could have been named for any of the above.

IOWA Street: The state was named for the Plains Indian tribe that originally inhabited the area that became the state.

IRIS Avenue: Named after either the flower or the mythological Greek goddess, who was the personification of the rainbow as well as the messenger of the gods.

IRONSHIP Plaza: Named after ships often found in Yerba Buena Cove, which is the present site of the Golden Gateway complex where this street is located. During the closing decades of the last century, American grain was the principal cargo of deepwater vessels sailing around Cape Horn to Europe. As many as 550 sailing ships were required to haul a single season's grain harvest; two-thirds of them were iron vessels from Britain. England started to construct iron sailing ships in the 1850s because the Napoleonic wars had exhausted its domestic supply of timber.

IRVING Street: Washington Irving (1783–1859) was called, among other things, "first American man of letters" and "Father of American literature." Irving's greatest literary success was *The Sketch Book*. This street is located near Hugo Street, while Goethe and Shakespeare streets are much farther south.

ISADORA DUNCAN Place: (formerly Adelaide Place) The birthplace of this famous dancer (1878–1927) is within a block of this alley. Seeking a more natural way to express herself through free-form movement, she was among the first to raise interpretive dance to the status of a creative art. Her death by strangulation occurred when the long scarf she was wearing got caught in one of the wheels of the car in which she was riding.

ISIS Street: The Isis, a clipper ship, brought pioneers to San Francisco. The name is taken from the ancient Egyptian goddess of fertility.

ITALY Avenue: The name comes from the *Itali* people—a primitive indigenous population who once lived in the eastern Italian region known as Lucania.

J

JACK KEROUAC Street: (formerly the western half of Adler Alley) Kerouac, the "King of the Beats," (1922–1969) first arrived in the Bay Area in 1947. He lived in North Beach, Russian Hill, and South of Market while he was writing his novels: *On the Road* (1951), *The Subterraneans* (1953), and *San Francisco Blues*. Two establishments—City Lights Bookstore and Vesuvio's Bar—often frequented by this legendary beatnik author, are still found in this alley.

JACK LONDON Street: (formerly Center Place) (1876–1916) Jack London was born a half block from where this street bisects South Park. His first story was published in 1898 in San Francisco's *Overland Monthly*. His first book, *The Son of Wolf*, was published two years later, and then he completed 50 books in the next 17 years. Although he became the highest paid writer in the United States, his expenditures always exceeded his earnings, and he was never free of the urgent need to write to earn money.

JACKSON Street: Andrew Jackson (1767–1845) was the seventh President of the United States and a military hero of the War of 1812. He was the first President from west of the Appalachians to be elected and the first to win office by a direct appeal to the voters. His political movement has since become known as "Jacksonian Democracy."

JAMESTOWN Avenue: Probably named for the first permanent British settlement in North America, founded on May 14, 1607, in Virginia. This community was named to honor King James I of England. Other possible sources for the name are: Jamestown, Rhode Island, which was named in honor of King James II, and Jamestown, New York, which was named after James Pendergast, who in 1811 selected the site for his mill, the nucleus of that community.

JANSEN Street: Possibly named for a pioneer merchant whose greatest claim to fame is that he was beaten and robbed in late February 1851. This and similar crimes eventually resulted in the creation of the Vigilance Committee, which established patrols against fire, theft, and other misdeeds. (See Coleman Street.)

JASON Court: According to Greek mythology, Jason was the leader of the Argonauts, sailors on the ship *Argo*. Jason was promised his inheritance if he accomplished a seemingly impossible task, acquiring the fabled Golden Fleece, a ram whose coat was made of gold. After many adventures, however, he was able to obtain the precious animal and to return home with it. Early San Franciscans were called Argonauts because of the hazardous and perilous journey they braved to reach California in search of gold. (See Argonaut Avenue.)

JAVA Street: Probably named after the fourth largest island in the Republic of Indonesia. East of Sumatra and west of Bali, this island was an important one to early San Francisco—all the West Coast's coffee came from Java, until a crop failure there forced Americans to turn to Costa Rica for their brew in the 1850s.

JEFFERSON Street: (Also Square) Probably named for Thomas Jefferson (1743–1826), the third President of the United States, the principal author of the Declaration of Independence, the first US Secretary of State, the founder of the University of Virginia, and an influential political leader and philosopher.

JENNINGS Street: Thomas Jennings, Sr., a San Francisco pioneer, was active in civic affairs. His son, Thomas, Jr., was a member of the Board of Supervisors in 1900–01 and again in 1908–09.

JERSEY Street: Probably named after the Jersey Islands in the English Channel that are governed by Great Britain.

JESSIE Street: This street name was selected by Immanuel Charles Christian Russ to honor a member of his family. He developed Russ Gardens, an amusement park, which was located downtown near this South of Market street.

JOAQUIN Street: A common Spanish name.

JOHN Street: Named after the disciple, who may well have been the author of the fourth book of the New Testament, the Gospel of St. John, as well as the three Epistles of John and the Revelation.

JOHN F. KENNEDY Drive: This thoroughfare in Golden Gate Park was originally called North Drive, but was renamed to honor the thirty-fifth President of the United States. Kennedy was the first Roman Catholic to become president. He launched the Peace Corps and the Alliance for Progress as well as outer space programs. He was assassinated on November 22, 1963.

JOHN MUIR Drive: A famous naturalist and conservationist, John Muir founded the Sierra Club in 1892. A native of Scotland, he spent his boyhood on a Wisconsin farm before moving to the West. Muir explored parts of Yosemite Valley and the High Sierra. He led a successful campaign to have Yosemite Valley and the surrounding highlands declared a national park.

JOICE Street: There are two possible sources for the origin of the name. One is John Joice, a land owner, about whom little is known other than that he sold a lot to James Lick in 1848. The other possibility is Erastus V. Joice, whose home once stood nearby at 807 Stockton. At one time he owned the Knickerbocker House Hotel and was reputed to have hunted in the area where this narrow street is located along Nob Hill. When elegant residences graced nearby Stockton Street, Joice Street was a service alley and stable entrance.

JONES Street: Probably named after Dr. Elbert P. Jones who was the first editor of the *California Star*, San Francisco's first newspaper. In addition to owning the second hotel building constructed in San Francisco, in 1847

he was elected to the first town council to serve under American jurisdiction. Or possibly named after Commodore Thomas A. Jones who
planted the first American flag on California soil when he captured
Monterey in 1842.

JOOST Avenue: In 1891 Behrend Joost built the electric streetcars which
connected Glen Park to the rest of San Francisco.

JORDAN Avenue: James Clark Jordan (1850–1910) once owned the Jordan tract, which was formerly the site of a race track and an area now
called Jordan Park. Born in Boston, Jordan graduated from Harvard and
entered his family's real-estate business. In the 1890s he moved to San
Francisco primarily for his health.

JOSEPHA Avenue: Josepha Petronila was the wife of a member of Captain Juan Anza's party, which came to what is now San Francisco in 1776.

JOY Street: The street next to this one is Faith; these streets were named
after basic human emotions and beliefs.

JUAN BAUTISTA Circle: Probably named for either Captain Juan Bautista
de Anza or for St. John the Baptist. (For a more complete biographical
description of Anza, see the entry under Anza Street.)

JUDAH Street: Born in Connecticut ,Theodore D. Judah arrived in San
Francisco in 1854 at the age of 28. A civil engineer, Judah constructed
California's first rail line, a 22 mile railroad from Sacramento to Folsom
and designed a railroad route over the Sierra Nevada. He was out-
maneuvered by the "Big Four," four clever Sacramento ex-merchants,
Stanford, Hopkins, Crocker, and Huntington. Judah consequently lost
his share of what was to become the Central Pacific Railroad to them.

JUDSON Street: The owner of a large South of Market estate, Egbert
Judson was the founder of the Judson Iron Works. He also bred cattle in
the 1870s.

JUNIPER Street: Probably named after the *Juniper*, a clipper ship which
brought pioneers to California.

JUNIPERO SERRA Boulevard: Father Junípero Serra established the first
mission in California in 1769. For many years, Serra served as the very
energetic and capable head of all the California missions.

JUSTIN Drive: Brother Justin was a leader of the Christian Brothers when
they came to take over St. Mary's College, which was once located near
this street. He was president of the college from 1868 to 1879. The
Christian Brothers order was founded by Jean Baptiste de La Salle
(1651–1719) to serve the poor and disenfranchised. Originally serving
Italian and Irish immigrants, today it is a lay order that focuses on
teaching.

KANSAS Street: The state's name comes from *Kansa* which is the Sioux language, means "people of the south wind."

KATE Street: A friend or relative of a pioneer.

KEARNY Street: During the beginning of the Mexican War of 1846–48, General Stephen Watts Kearny was placed in command of an expedition from Ft. Leavenworth, Kansas, whose mission was to conquer and occupy New Mexico and California. In 1847 he was appointed the military and civil governor of California. On this street, the world's first cable car made its first public trip on June 28, 1873. Along with Montgomery, Washington, and Clay—the names of other streets—Kearny has been in continuous usage as a street name longer than any other in San Francisco. In 1854 the portion of Kearny Street between Washington and Clay Streets was paved, making it the City's first paved street.

KENNETH REXROTH Place: (formerly Tracy Place) Kenneth Rexroth was one of the most important of the numerous critics, philosophers, and poets to live in San Francisco in the post-World War II period. Moreover, he was one of the first American abstract painters and a prolific translator of Japanese, Chinese, Greek, Latin, and Spanish poetry. Off and on in the 1930s, he resided not far from this North Beach alley.

KENSINGTON Way: Probably named after Kensington, England.

KENWOOD Way: One of a series of streets in Westwood Highlands, which all have the suffix of "wood."

KEY Avenue: Francis Scott Key was a lawyer and the author of the lyrics to the United States national anthem, the "Star-Spangled Banner." He died in 1843 at the age of 64.

KEYES Avenue: (also Alley) Brigadier General Erasmus D. Keyes was the commanding officer of the Presidio for the six years starting in November 1849, and then again from October 1856 to June 1858.

KEZAR Drive: Mary A. Kezar gave $100,000 to the City in 1923 to erect a stadium in Golden Gate Park that was subsequently named after her. The facility was completed in 1926 and then remodeled in 1991.

KING Street: Probably named for T. Butler King, who arrived in 1847. He was an agent for the United States to California before it became a part of the Union. Or possibly it was named in honor of James King, a successful banker, and later in his career, a crusading newspaper editor, who was shot in the street by James P. Casey, a San Francisco supervisor and former in-mate of Sing Sing Prison. Casey had been angered by a muckraking series in King's newspaper which exposed Casey's efforts to stuff the ballot box. Casey, along with gambler Charles Cora, was hanged by an angry mob on the day King was buried. (See Cora Street.)

KINGSTON Street: Possibly named after the city in New York state or the borough in Pennsylvania. Both of these communities, as well as others with the same name, were named after Kingston-upon-Thames, a royal borough in London. In turn, this name was derived from the Saxon word *cyningestun,* or "king's town."

KIRKHAM Street: A member of the Quartermaster Corps, Brigadier General Ralph W. Kirkham fought in the Mexican War of 1847 and the Civil War.

KIRKWOOD Avenue: Samuel J. Kirkwood was an early governor of Iowa.

KISSLING Street: Kissling once owned property in the South of Market area where this street is located.

KNOLLVIEW Way: One of a series of streets with the suffix of "view" in Midtown Terrace, a residential subdivision on the northwest slope of Twin Peaks.

KOBBE Avenue: Major General William A. Kobbe was once an artillery officer at the Presidio.

KOHALA Road: This volcanic mountain range is situated on the northern part of the island of Hawaii.

KRAMER Place: In 1856 Jacob Kramer operated a grocery store in the vicinity of this North Beach street. After he died, his family continued operating the business until the fire of 1906.

KRONQUIST Court: He was one of the developers of this part of Noe Valley.

LA AVANZADA: In Spanish this word means "a group of soldiers which advances to observe the enemy at close range."

LA BICA Way: *Bica* is a kind of cornbread eaten in Mexico.

LA GRANDE Avenue: The name of this street belies the fact that it is only one block long.

LAFAYETTE Street: General Marquis de Lafayette was an American Revolutionary hero (1757–1834). Born into a noble French family, Lafayette aspired to glory as a soldier. He came to America to help the colonists in the Revolution. Lafayette became friends with General George Washington and persuaded Louis XIV to send a 6,000-man expeditionary army to aid the American rebels.

LAGUNA Street: This is Spanish for "lagoon." At one time, a small lake known as Washerwoman's Lagoon existed one-half mile southwest of Fort Mason. In early times, most of the laundry for the San Francisco was done there. Today Laguna Street runs into the Bay at this site, now known as Gashouse Cove.

LAGUNA HONDA Boulevard: In Spanish, this means "deep lagoon." The street runs next to a reservoir at the edge of Sutro Forest where there was once a deep lake. Actually, the street was named after the Laguna Honda Home which was named for the lake.

LAGUNITAS Drive: This word in Spanish means "little lakes."

LAKE Street: Named after Mountain Lake which is next to this street at 12th Avenue.

LAKE FOREST Court: Situated in Forest Knolls, a subdivision on the slopes of Mt. Sutro where some of the streets have sylvan names. This street reminds one of neither the famed Chicago suburb nor a body of water.

LAKE MERCED Boulevard: This lake was named by the Spanish, *Laguna de Nuestra Señora de la Merced*, literally, "Lake of our Lady of Mercy."

LAKE MERCED HILLS North/South: Named after Lake Merced (see above).

LAKESHORE Drive: (also Plaza) This street derives its name from the fact that it follows the shoreline of Lake Merced.

LAKEVIEW Avenue: This street has no view of a lake now, but it might have had a view when Lake Geneva, which is now gone, was at the corner of Niagara and Delano Streets.

LAKEWOOD Avenue: Neither a lake nor a wood is evident from this street, but a large number of bottlebrush trees provide a sylvan setting for this thoroughfare, which is situated in Westwood Highlands, where many streets have the suffix of wood.

LANE Street: Doctor L. C. Lane, a prominent physician, founded Cooper Medical School, which became the Stanford Medical School and is now the Pacific Medical Center.

LAPHAM Way: Roger Dearborn Lapham (1883–1966) served as the thirty-second mayor of San Francisco from 1944 to 1948. When elected he said, "four years will be long enough." A graduate of Harvard, he worked for, and eventually became president of, the family-organized and owned American Hawaiian Steamship Company. Lapham Way is adjacent to a street named for the thirty-third mayor, Elmer Robinson.

LA PLAYA: Spanish for "beach," this is an appropriate name since this street probably used to run along the beach. Sand dunes still abut this thoroughfare.

LAPU LAPU Street: In 1521 this Filipino hero's army repulsed the invasion of the Spanish explorer, Ferdinand Magellan, who was killed when he and his conquistadors landed in the Philippines. The street name was changed in 1979 from Maloney Street to Lapu Lapu in recognition of the growing Filipino community, the area south of Market Street.

LARKIN Street: Multi-talented Thomas O. Larkin arrived in California in 1831 and had a store in Monterey for many years. Larkin was the first and only consul to the Mexican government; he was also a secret agent for the United States, who tried to arrange an American occupation of California without a war. A California correspondent for several New York newspapers, Larkin was a central figure in the first State constitutional convention.

LA SALLE Avenue: Robert Cavalier, Sieur de la Salle (1643–1687) was a French explorer who claimed to have discovered the Ohio River. La Salle established France's claim of ownership of Louisiana and the Mississippi Valley.

LATHROP Avenue: Possibly named after Leland Stanford's brother-in-law, Charles Lathrop. Leland Stanford was one of the "Big Four" who built the Central Pacific Railroad. The "Big Four" were four prosperous Sacramento ex-merchants who invested in this railroad venture and became even more wealthy in the process.

LATONA Avenue: This is the Latin name for Leto, who, in classical Greek mythology, was the goddess of fertility and the mother of Artemis and Apollo. (Apollo Street is seven blocks away.)

LAURA Street: (See Petrarch Place.)

LAWTON Street: Brigadier General Henry W. Lawton became the military Governor of Santiago, Cuba after its surrender in the Spanish-American War. In 1886, Lawton led troops into Mexico and captured the Apache Chief Geronimo.

LECH WALESA Street: The block of Ivy Street between Van Ness and Polk was renamed Lech Walesa to honor the Polish Solidarity leader who became his nation's president in 1990. Walesa is the only foreign Nobel Peace Prize recipient to be honored with a street name in San Francisco, and the only Pole to ever receive the Nobel Peace Prize, which he was awarded twice.

LE CONTE Avenue: Professor John Le Conte, teacher, scientist, and author, served as the third president of the University of California. After teaching extensively in eastern colleges, Le Conte moved to Berkeley where he was the University of California's first faculty member. A professor of physics, Le Conte was president of the University from 1869 to 1870 and again from 1875 to 1881.

LEAVENWORTH Street: The Reverend Thaddeu M. Leavenworth was an Episcopalian minister, physician, and pharmacist who served as a chief magistrate in 1848–49.

LEE Avenue: Presumed to be named for Lieutenant Curtis Lee, a son of Robert E. Lee. Curtis Lee was an aide to General Clark when he commanded the US Army's Department of California.

LEESE Street: Jacob Primer Leese built the first permanent house in Yerba Buena on the block bounded by Grant, Sacramento, Clay, and Stockton Streets in 1836. Leese was a merchant and a large property holder. He married Vallejo's sister, and probably because of this fact, Leese was taken prisoner with Vallejo during the Bear Flag Revolt and held captive at Sutter's Fort. (See Vallejo Street.)

LEGION OF HONOR Drive: This drive enters Lincoln Park at 34th Avenue and Clement and leads to the museum "the Palace of the Legion of Honor," which was named after a building in Paris. The original building in Paris was built by Napoleon to honor his military forces.

LEIDESDORFF Street: William A. Leidesdorff, a black man, was born in the Danish West Indies and raised by a wealthy plantation owner. In 1841, Leidesdorff arrived in San Francisco and became one of the City's most enterprising and public-spirited citizens. A merchant and land owner, Leidesdorff served as captain of the port. He built the first hotel, the City Hotel, and was appointed vice consul at Yerba Buena in 1845. He also served as city treasurer, a member of the School Board, and one of the first Municipal Council members, as well as the Russian consul. Leidesdorff operated the first steamer on the Bay—the Russian ship *Sitka*.

LENDRUM Court: Captain John H. Lendrum was the commanding officer of the Presidio in 1858, and the first commander of Fort Point in 1861.

LENOX Way: Named possibly for Lenox, Massachusetts, which was probably named for one of several Charles Lenoxes, the Dukes of Richmond.

LEXINGTON Street: In this Massachusetts town the first battle of the Revolutionary War was fought on April 9, 1775. Seventy-seven minutemen took their positions on the Lexington green to resist the British force of 700 men. The Massachusetts town was named for Laxton, England.

LIBERTY Street: After the Civil War, those naming the City's streets were caught in a burst of patriotism and sought to find appropriate words, such as this one, to express their feelings.

LICK Place: An eccentric Pennsylvanian, James Lick worked his way to San Francisco via South America by selling pianos. He arrived just before the Gold Rush with about $30,000. Intent on accumulating a larger fortune, Lick invested in what was then outlying San Francisco real estate. Some of his investments included a fruit orchard in the Santa Clara Valley, a flour mill in the San Jose area, and Lick House, a famous restaurant and hotel in its day. As a result of these ventures, when he died, Lick was very wealthy; he left several million dollars for scientific, charitable, and educational purposes. The Lick Observatory atop Mount Hamilton and the Lick Wilmerding School in San Francisco exist because of his philanthropy.

LIGGETT Avenue: Lieutenant General Hunter Liggett was the commanding officer of the Western Department of the US Army from May 1914, until September 1917, and was commanding officer of the Ninth Corps from August 1919 until March 1921. In 1923 this street was named to honor him.

LILLIAN Street: Lillian Wood was a prominent community leader in Hunters Point during the 1960s when the Redevelopment Agency's project was being developed there.

LINARES Avenue: He was a soldier in Captain Juan Anza's party, which came to northern California in 1776.

LINCOLN Boulevard, Court, and Way: Abraham Lincoln (1809–1865), sixteenth President of the United States, preserved the Union during the American Civil War and emancipated the slaves. Lincoln was assassinated by John Wilkes Booth shortly after the Union victory.

LINDA Street: In Spanish, *linda* means "pretty," but this was probably the name of a woman who was a friend of a contractor or a politician.

LISBON Street: Most historians believe that the name for the Portuguese capital city is probably derived from *água boa* or "good water."

LOBOS Street: In Spanish, this word literally means "wolves," but along the California coast the word has also been applied to sea lions.

LOEHR Street: Ferdinand Loehr was the editor of the *California Democrat* (a German language newspaper), and he was also a physician.

LOMA VISTA Terrace: The Spanish geographical term *loma* designates a "long, little hill." *Vista* means "view" in Spanish. There is a view of the City from some of the homes on this short street located off of an approach to Mt. Olympus.

LOMBARD Street: Named by Jasper O'Farrell for the street of the same name in Philadelphia, which got its name from London's financial street. The name is originally derived from the Italian moneylenders of Genoa and Florence, the Lombards. A Germanic people, the Lombards founded Lombardy in northern Italy in 568 A.D. One source asserts that these people got their name from their long, uncut beards. The block of this street between Hyde and Leavenworth Street has been called "the crookedest street in the world." In 1923 eight turns were fashioned on this one block of Lombard Street.

LOMITA Avenue: The Mexican or Spanish diminutive of *loma* meaning "little hill." Las Lomitas was the name given to Yerba Buena by the early Spaniards.

LONDON Street: The capital of the United Kingdom, the center of the Commonwealth of Nations, and Great Britain's largest port and industrial complex, London is Britain's principal financial, commercial, and cultural center. In Roman times this city was known as Londinium.

LONE MOUNTAIN Terrace: Named for the mountain, which is distinct and separate from San Francisco's other mountains.

LONGVIEW Court: One of a series of streets in Midtown Terrace, a residential subdivision on the northwest slope of Twin Peaks, which have the suffix "view."

LOPEZ Avenue: A member of Captain Juan Anza's 1776 party to northern California, Lopez was one of the first settlers in San Francisco.

LOTTIE BENNETT Lane: An appropriate name for a street in a housing project sponsored by the International Longshoremen's Union. The *Lottie Bennett* was a four-masted schooner built at Point Blakely, Washington, in 1899.

LOUISBURG Street: Named possibly after a square on Beacon Hill in Boston.

LOWER Terrace: One of two such streets—the other one is Upper Terrace—on the slopes of Mt. Olympus, whose names give a verbal sense of their spatial relationship.

LOYOLA Terrace: This street was named for St. Ignatius of Loyola (1491–1556). His name comes from his home town—Loyola, Spain. St. Ignatius was one of the most influential figures in the Catholic Reformation and founded the Society of Jesus, the Jesuits, in 1534. This street is next to the campus of the University of San Francisco, the City's first university and a distinguished Jesuit institution.

LUCERNE Street: Probably named after the lake or city in Switzerland, which may have been the home town of a pioneer. The name is derived from the Benedictine monastery of St. Leodezar (Luciara) in Switzerland, which was founded in the Eighth Century.

LUNADO Court: (also Way) Derived from the Spanish word *luna* meaning "moon." *Lunado* means "crescent-shaped."

LUNDY'S Lane: Occurring a mile west of Niagara Falls, in Canada, the Battle of Lundy's Lane took place on July 25, 1814. It ended the United States' invasion of Canada during the War of 1812.

LURLINE Street: The *Lurline* was one of the most popular tourist ships that journeyed between San Francisco and Hawaii. The street was named after the ship in order to capitalize on the allure of the islands.

LYON Street: A West Point graduate, Captain Nathaniel Lyon fought in the Mexican War. In California, Lyon was active in campaigns against the Indians. He was killed in the Civil War.

MABINI Street: A Filipino theoretician and spokesman for the Philippine Revolution, Mabini wrote the constitution for the short-lived republic which existed in these islands in 1898–99. Prior to 1979 this street was called Alice Street.

MACARTHUR Avenue: Lieutenant General Arthur MacArthur was commander of the US Army in the Department of California in 1903–05. He also served in the Civil War and the Spanish-American War. He was awarded a Medal of Honor for bravery. He was the father of General Douglas MacArthur, the famed general during World War II.

MACEDONIA Street: The name is derived from Macedonis, the Bishop of Constantinople in the middle of the Fourth Century. He was deposed for suggesting a new view of the Holy Trinity. Those who accepted his somewhat heretical view were called Macedonians. In general, they resided in the central part of the Balkan peninsula lying astride the frontiers of Macedonia (formerly southern Yugoslavia), northern Greece, and southwest Bulgaria.

MACONDRAY Lane: A son of a Scottish sea captain, Frederick William Macondray arrived in San Francisco in 1849. After an early career at sea, he established the large mercantile firm of Macondray and Co.

MADERA Street: The California county was named for the Spanish word for "wood," and it is an appropriate name for this street which ends in a park.

MADISON Street: Probably named for James Madison (1751–1836), the fourth President of the United States. Madison is also known as the "Father of the United States Constitution." Prior to serving as president, Madison was Jefferson's Secretary of State for eight years.

MADRID Street: The capital of Spain is the highest in elevation of the European capital cities (2,100 ft.). Declared the official capital in 1607, Madrid was the seat of a succession of Spanish kings who ruled from here. It developed a rich cultural and architectural heritage. The name is probably derived from an earlier time when a small Moorish fort called Majrit was located on the site. This fort was a part of the outlying defenses of Toledo, 40 miles to the southwest.

MADRONE Avenue: This broad-leaved evergreen shrub or tree grows along the Pacific Coast from British Columbia to southern California.

MAGELLAN Avenue: Named for a member of the Gaspar de Portolá expedition, *not* after Ferdinand Magellan, the famed explorer.

MAIDEN Lane: In 1922, Alfred Samuels, a local jeweler, suggested this name, probably after the name of a street in New York's jewelry center, whose namesake, in turn, was derived from a pebbly brook that once ran into New York's East River. The gentle grassy slope of the stream's bank provided an ideal spot for bleaching and washing clothes, a chore undertaken in most families by young girls or maidens. There is also a Maiden Lane near Covenant Gardens in London, which also might have served as an inspiration for Samuel's nomenclature since it is the site of the London diamond district. In the years before it became Maiden Lane, this short San Francisco street was called Morton Alley, then Union Square Alley, and later, Manila, to link it to the Dewey Monument in nearby Union Square. During some of those years when it was Morton Alley, the street was the location of low class brothels or "cribs," thus suggesting a somewhat misguided origin for its name.

MAIN Street: Charles Main sailed from Boston to San Francisco via Cape Horn on a voyage which lasted five months and one day in 1845. Main began his career as a miner, but soon switched to manufacturing, wholesaling, and retailing leather saddleware, a business in which he became very successful. For several years, Main was the president and director

MACONDRAY Lane

of the Central Railroad of San Francisco and of the Geary Street Wire-rope Railroad Company. He was also a founder and director of the California Insurance Company and a director of several banks. Main was instrumental in securing the passage of a bill which widened Kearny Street from Market Street to Broadway.

MAJESTIC Avenue: The view from the south end of this street, looking towards Twin Peaks and the San Francisco Bay, is majestic.

MALLORCA Way: This Spanish island is the largest one in the western Mediterranean Balearic chain.

MALTA Drive: Named after the country of Malta, which is situated on several islands in the central Mediterranean Sea. It became independent in 1964, long after this street received its name.

MANCHESTER Street: Probably named for the manufacturing city in England, which was named by the Romans when they built a fort on the site of the existing city (78–86 A.D.). They named the fort Mamucium, place of the breastlike hill.

MANZANITA Avenue: In Spanish, this means "little apple," since it is the diminutive of *manzana*. This native shrub of California mountain areas has red berries resembling apples, hence the Spanish name.

MARENGO Street: The Battle of Marengo took place on June 14, 1800, in northern Italy, where Napoleon's troops narrowly defeated the Austrian army. The victory secured Napoleon's military and civilian authority in France. Napoleon Street is located nearby.

MARIN Street: Named for Marin County, which was probably named for Chief Marin of the Licatiut Indians, a tribe of the Coastal Miwok. This Miwok chief was captured and then baptized *Marinero* or "sailor" because he was an excellent navigator. Later, he was the first ferryman on San Francisco Bay. (For an expanded explanation of the origin of this name see also Marin in the Bay Area Landmarks section of this book.)

MARINA Boulevard: This is the Spanish word for "seacoast."

MARIPOSA Street: Named after the county which, in turn, was named for the Spanish word for "butterfly."

MARK Lane: Named to honor Mark Aldrich (1801–1873). Although Aldrich's life was colorful, no one knows why a street was named for him. Born in New York, he moved to Illinois and was elected to the state legislature in 1836. In 1845, in the town of Nauvoo, Illinois, he was tried and acquitted of murdering the visionary founder of the Mormons, Joseph Smith, and Smith's brother Hyrum, and of wounding follower John Taylor. Aldrich deserted his family in 1850 and headed for the Gold Rush. Aldrich Street is also named after him.

MARKET Street: This main thoroughfare was laid out by Jasper O'Farrell, the City's civil engineer in 1846. It ran from the waterfront to Twin Peaks; paralleling much of the Old Mission Trail, the first road between the village of Yerba Buena and Mission Dolores. George Hyde, another City official and a Philadelphian, may have suggested the street be named after the major east/west street in his hometown. Philadelphia's Market Street was originally called High Street. By 1759, however, the name was changed because the street served that city's market. San Francisco's Market Street crosses through the City at a forty-five degree angle, thus causing much confusion for motorists, pedestrians, and property owners.

MARK TWAIN Lane: (formerly the western end of Merchant Street) At this site, which was the former location of the Montgomery Building (Monkey Block) and is now the east side of the Transamerica pyramid, Mark Twain (1836–1910) met a man named Tom Sawyer, whose name he adopted for his most famous novel. Mark Twain, whose real name was Samuel Clemens, was a humorist, writer, newspaperman, and lecturer who earned a worldwide audience for his stories of the boyhood of Tom Sawyer and Huckleberry Finn. Twain moved to San Francisco in 1863. While here, he was a reporter for the *Daily Morning Call* and a columnist for a literary journal, the *Golden Era*, whose offices were just north of the Montgomery Block. He also wrote for the *Dramatic Chronicle* and the *Californian*.

MARS Street: This ancient Roman god was second only to Jupiter in importance. In Roman literature, Mars was the god of war and protector of Rome. Mars Street runs next to Uranus Street, which intersects Saturn Street. All these thoroughfares are located on the slopes of Mt. Olympus.

MARSILLY Street:. The De Boom family once owned the tract of land on which this street is located. Mrs. Roman De Boom's maiden name was Marsilly.

MARTIN LUTHER KING, JR. Drive: In December 1983, South Drive was renamed to honor the slain civil rights leader. Located in Golden Gate Park, this street is positioned between John F. Kennedy Drive and Lincoln Way. Martin Luther King, Jr. was the winner of the Nobel Peace Prize in 1964 for his leadership of nonviolent resistance in the struggle for racial equality. This eloquent, Afro-American, Baptist minister will long be remembered for his speech, "I Have A Dream," delivered in 1963 during a massive demonstration in Washington, D.C.

MARVIEW Way: "A view of the sea" in Spanish/English. This is one of a number of streets with the suffix of "view" in Midtown Terrace, a residential subdivision on the slope of Twin Peaks.

MARY Street: Named for a friend or relative of a pioneer.

MASON Street: Colonel Richard B. Mason was the military governor of California from May 1847 to February 1849. In the summer of 1848, Mason made an inspection of the gold district and sent the famous report to Washington, D.C. that, along with letters from Thomas Larkin, started the big rush to California the following year. Two "Mason" streets are found in San Francisco, one downtown, the other in the Presidio.

MASONIC Avenue: This street originally ran next to the Masonic cemetery which was operated by the fraternal order. The English word "mason" is from the French *maçon* which means "bricklayer."

MATEO Street: This Spanish word means "Matthew" in English. (See San Mateo Avenue.)

MAYWOOD Drive: One of a number of streets in Westwood Highlands with the suffix of "wood."

McALLISTER Street: An attorney and distinguished jurist, Hall McAllister was referred to as "the most eminent lawyer in California" during the Gold Rush period. It is said that in 1849 McAllister gave either $35 or a bottle of champagne to a City official in return for the promise of having a street named after him. He is also reputed to have gambled away his home on the turn of a single card. In the same year, McAllister won fame by having the notorious "Hounds" convicted. This was a group of former criminals who professed to believe in law and order but actually were intent on continuing their old behavior.

McCARTHY Avenue: Constructed in the late 1960s or early 1970s, this street may have been named for either Peter or James McCarthy. The latter is more likely. James was San Francisco's third planning director. In the early 1960s he worked closely with Joseph Eichler, the developer of Argonaut Place, which abuts this street. Peter, a newspaper distributor, was an early settler in Visitacion Valley where this street is situated. His daughter, Kate, married Ted Schwerin, whose father and mother both had streets named for them.

McCOPPIN Street: Frank H. McCoppin was the ninth mayor of San Francisco, serving from 1867 to 1869. In 1860, McCoppin was general manager of the Old Market Street Railroad Co., which ran steam trains on Market Street, the City's first mechanical public transportation.

McKINNON Avenue: Father McKinnon was the chaplain of the First California Volunteers in the Spanish-American War. He died in the Philippines.

McLAREN Avenue: A Scotsman, John McLaren was superintendent of Golden Gate Park for almost 56 years. A master horticulturist, McLaren transformed the windswept sand dunes, and the rest of the 1,017-acre park, into the largest and most beautiful man-made park in the world. He died in his nineties, in 1943.

MEADE Avenue: General George G. Meade (1815–1872) played a critical role in the Civil War by leading the Union forces in the defeat of the Confederate Army at Gettysburg in July 1863. Meade repulsed Lee's forces with great tactical skill; however, he has been criticized by some for allowing Lee's army to escape after this decisive victory.

MELBA Avenue: Probably named after Dame Nellie Melba, for whom a toast and dessert were also named. She was an operatic soprano, famed for her performances of coloratura roles in the latter part of the last century and first quarter of this one. She was born Helen Mitchell near Melbourne, Australia—her stage name is derived from this city's name.

MENDELL Street: A member of the Army Corps of Engineers, Colonel George H. Mendell directed many Pacific Coast defenses. In San Francisco, Mendell served as president of the Board of Public Works from 1900 to 1903.

MENDOSA Avenue: Antonio de Mendosa was the Spanish Viceroy in Mexico City and the superior officer under whom the Coronado and Cabrillo expeditions were made.

MERCED Avenue: This Spanish word means "mercy." "The Lady of Mercy" is the Virgin Mary.

MERCEDES Way: The word is derived from the Spanish word which means "mercy." It is a common Spanish girl's name.

MERCHANT Street: Brigadier General Charles S. Merchant served in the War of 1812, and he was the commanding officer of the Presidio twice.

MERCURY Street: Mercury was the Roman god of merchandise and merchants. He is usually represented as standing and holding a purse, which is symbolic of his business functions. Mercury is also the name of a planet. This street is situated near Venus and Neptune streets.

MERSEY Street: Probably named after the river in England which flows past Liverpool down to the Irish Sea.

MESA Street: (Also Avenue) Named in honor of Alfrez Juan Prado Mesa, acting-commanding officer of the Presidio in 1835, 1839, and 1843.

MICHIGAN Street: This state is the only one of the 49 continental states to be split into two large land segments, both of which are peninsulas. The name is from an Indian word of uncertain origin. One theory claims derivation from *mitchisawgyegan*, a combination of Indian words meaning "great lake" (presumably Lake Michigan). Another suggests *mishimaikin-nac*, "swimming turtle," an Indian term used to describe the profile of the northern tip of the southern peninsula and a nearby island. It is unclear which was named first, the lake or the land area.

MIDCREST Way: An appropriate name for a street which is located near the top of Twin Peaks.

MIDDLE Drive: This road in Golden Gate Park lies between what was once North Drive and South Drive. Now, however, North Drive has been renamed John F. Kennedy Drive and South Drive has been renamed Martin Luther King, Jr. Drive.

MIDDLE POINT Road: This street lies between West Point Road and Hunters Point Road.

MIDWAY Street: This street lies halfway between Stockton and Grant streets and connects Francisco Street with Bay Street.

MILAN Terrace: Probably named after the city in northern Italy, which is a leading financial, industrial, and commercial center. At the time of the Roman Conquest in 222 B.C., the town was called Mediolanum.

MILEY Street: Probably named in honor of Lieutenant Colonel John D. Miley who died in Manila in 1899, during the Spanish-American War. Fort Miley, located in the northeast corner of the City near lands End, is also named for this officer.

MINERVA Street: Minerva was the Roman goddess of handicrafts, professions, arts, and, later, war.

MINNA Street: Probably named for a pioneer.

MINNESOTA Street: The state was named for the river which flows into the Mississippi River near the state capital of St. Paul. The name of the river is derived from a Dakota (Sioux) Indian word. While scholars agree that *minne* means "water," there is a difference of opinion on the meaning when *minne* is joined with *sota*. The majority of scholars think that *sota* refers to "the reflection of the sky upon the water," but some think that the two words together, *minnesota*, mean "water reflecting cloudy skies."

MINT Street: This street is next to the second United States branch mint in California. The building survived the earthquake and fire of 1906. The first mint was located on Commercial Street between Montgomery and Kearny streets.

MIRALOMA Drive: This is Spanish for "hill view."

MIRAMAR Avenue: This Spanish word means "sea view."

MIRANDO Way: *Mirando* means "looking" in Spanish.

MISSION Street: The longest (7.29 miles) and one of the oldest streets in San Francisco, this road follows the original trail which linked the village of Yerba Buena with Mission Dolores. Originally a toll road, it was planked for two-and-one-half miles starting at Third Street.

MISSION ROCK Street: This street lies on the approach to Mission Rock ship terminal, which was named for the large rock in Mission Bay. This bay comprised the San Francisco waterfront from China Basin to Central Basin before it was filled in. There was also a Mission Creek which fed into Mission Bay. All these places take their name from Mission Dolores.

MISSISSIPPI Street: Named for either the state or the river that flows along most of the state's western border. The river was named by the Algonquian speaking Indians and they called it the "Father of Waters." It is derived from *meeche* or *mescha*, meaning "great," and *cebe*, meaning "river" or "water."

MISSOURI Street: The state got its name from the river that bisects it. The river was given its name by French explorers who named it after a tribe who inhabited an area near the mouth of the river. On some early French maps this river was originally named *Peki-tan-oui* or *Pokitanou*, which means "muddy water," but later it was named *Oomessourit*.

MIZPAH Street: Mizpah is the biblical town, whose name in Hebrew means "of Benjamin." This city is north of Jerusalem in Israel.

MODOC Avenue: This word, which means "southerners," was used by the Klamath Indians when speaking of the tribe which lived south of them. It is also the name of a county in northeastern California near where the Klamath Indians once lived.

MOJAVE Street: Named after the desert and river of the same name. The name is an Hispanicized phonetic rendering of the name of a Yuman Indian tribe that was first called Jamajah by Franciscan missionary explorer Brother Francisco Garcés in 1775. The name is more accurately rendered in English as Hamakhava. (See also Garcés Drive.)

MONCADA Way: Fernando Rivera y Moncada was second in command to Portolá, Governor of California, from 1773 to 1777. Rivera Street was also named for him. Moncada opposed the early settlement of Yerba Buena (now San Francisco), preferring that new settlers expand the small population base of the capital at Monterey. Quarreling with Anza, he ordered his lieutenant, Moraga, to establish only a presidio and not a mission, but these instructions were ignored. Moncada was killed by Yuma Indians in 1781. (See also Garcés Drive.)

MONO Street: Named for the Shoshone-speaking Indian tribe of Central California. There were two branches, the eastern and western, that traded with each other. The latter group lived in the pine belt of the Sierra Nevada, while the former lived east of the Sierra crest near Mono Lake.

MONTALVO Avenue: García Ordóñez de Montalvo was the author of *Las Sèrgas de Esplandián*, in which the word "California" first appeared.

MONTECITO Avenue: This Spanish word means "little mountain."

MONTEREY Boulevard: The city and county were named in honor of Gaspar de Zuñiga, Count of Monterey and Viceroy of Mexico.

MONTEZUMA Street: The legendary leader and last emperor of the Aztecs in Mexico during the Spanish conquest, Montezuma became famous for his dramatic confrontation with Hernán Cortés, the Spanish conquistador. The adjacent street is Aztec Street.

MONTGOMERY Street: Captain John B. Montgomery received orders from Commodore Sloat to occupy the little town of Yerba Buena for the United States on July 9, 1846. Montgomery landed seventy men from his boat, the USS *Portsmouth*, and raised the American flag on land amid, "the roar of cannon from the ship, and hurrahs of the ship's company, the vivas of the Californians, the cheers of the Dutchmen, the barking of dogs, braying of jackasses, and a general confusion of sounds from every living thing within hearing" as one spectator later wrote. Montgomery remained in command of the district for five months. Along with Kearny, Washington, and Clay—the names of other streets—Montgomery, as a street name, has been in continuous usage longer than any others in San Francisco. Two such streets now exist in San Francisco, one in the downtown financial district, the other in the Presidio.

MONTICELLO Street: Italian for "little hill."

MORAGA Avenue: (Also Street) Lieutenant José Joaquin Moraga was second in command of the Anza expedition in 1776. Left in command at the Presidio when building started there, he remained the first commanding officer until July 1785. Moraga also played a leading role in the construction of Mission Dolores and the Santa Clara Mission as well as in the establishment of the town of San Jose.

MORNINGSIDE Drive: Possibly named after the street of the same name in New York City. In turn, this street was named for the park which it borders. The park in New York occupies the eastern or morning side of a rocky elevation which acts as Harlem's western border.

MORRIS Street: George R. Morris operated a store in China Camp in Marin County in the 1850s and 1860s. He died defending his business during a robbery.

MOSCOW Street: The capital and largest city in Russia is Moscow, which is on the river of the same name.

MOSS Street: In 1850, J. Mora Moss (1807–1880) came to San Francisco from his native Philadelphia. Soon Moss was affiliated with the banking firm of Pioche and Bayesque and the Alaska Fur Company. He was the first president and a major stockholder of the San Francisco Gas Company. A member of the board of directors of the Deaf and Dumb Asylum, Moss was also appointed a Regent of the University of California in 1868 and was reappointed in 1874.

MOULTRIE Street: The fort in Charleston, South Carolina, was named to honor William Moultrie, a native of that area who resisted the British incursions into the South during the War of Independence. After the war, he served two terms as governor of his state.

MT. SUTRO Drive: The mountain was named for Adolph Sutro, the twenty-first mayor of San Francisco. (See Sutro Heights Avenue.)

MOUNT VERNON Avenue: Probably named after the home and burial place of George Washington. The homesite was named by Washington's older half-brother, Lawrence, to honor his former British commander, Admiral Edward Vernon, under whom he had served in the Caribbean.

MOUNTAIN VIEW Court: With a view of Twin Peaks, this is an appropriate name for this street, one of a number with the suffix of "view" in Midtown Terrace, a residential subdivision located on the slope of these hills.

MUNICH Street: The third largest German city is the capital of Bavaria. The German word for this city is *München* which means "home of the monks."

MUSEUM Way: The museum is the Josephine D. Randall Junior Museum; this road leads to it.

N

NANTUCKET Avenue: Nantucket is an island situated 25 miles off Cape Cod and 15 miles east of Martha's Vineyard. Nantucket was the Native American word for "far away land."

NAPIER Lane: Here, on the slope of Telegraph Hill, one finds the last wooden sidewalk and some of the oldest houses in San Francisco. Legend has it that, in these homes, sailors were drugged, then kidnapped, and put onto vessels as crew members. Who Napier was, remains a mystery.

NAPLES Street: The Italian word for this city is Napoli. In ancient times it was called *Neapolis*, or "New Town." In Greek *polis* means "town" or "city." From the Middle Ages to 1860, Napoli was the capital of the Kingdom of Naples which occupied the southern part of the Italian peninsula.

NAPOLEON Street: Napoleon Bonaparte, the French general and emperor, (1769–1821) is one of the most celebrated personages in the history of the Western Europe. He temporarily extended French domination over a large part of Europe, leaving a lasting mark on the lands he ruled. Waterloo Street is nearby.

NATICK Street: Probably named after the Scottish hometown of a contractor named Allen, who probably wanted to honor his birthplace. (See Allen street.)

NATOMA Street: Named after an Indian tribe on the American and Feather rivers in the vicinity of the town of Natomas. The Indian name has several translations: one version gives the meaning as "the girl from the mountains," while another version suggests direction and is interpreted to mean "up-stream."

NAUTILUS Street: Probably named after the mollusk or the chambered machine of Oliver Wendell Holmes' poetic fancy.

NAVAJO Avenue: This tribe is currently the most populous of all Indian groups in the United States with about 200,000 individuals scattered throughout northwestern New Mexico, northeastern Arizona, and southeastern Utah.

NAVY Road: This aptly named road goes to the naval shipyards at Hunters Point.

NEBRASKA Street: The state's name is derived from two different Indian words meaning "flat water"—a reference to both the Platte and Nebraska rivers. The Omaha Indian name for these rivers is *Niubthatka*; the Oto Indian name for them is *Nebrathka*.

NEPTUNE Street: In Roman mythology, Neptune was the god of fresh water, not the sea; however, he is usually thought of as the god of the sea because he is identified with the Greek sea god, Poseidon. This is one of a series of streets in the Bay View district named after Roman gods. Neptune is near Venus and Saturn Streets, which are also the names of planets.

NEVADA Street: The state's name is a shortened form of *Sierra Nevada*, a mountain range that runs through western Nevada and eastern California, which was named for the range in southern Spain. In Spanish *sierra* means "mountain range," and *nevada* means "snowcovered."

NEWBURG Street: A short street possibly named for either the city in New York or the one in Scotland. *Burg* is German for "town," hence the name means "new town."

NEWCOMB Avenue: Simon Newcomb (1835–1909) was a distinguished astronomer and mathematician who prepared ephemerides—tables of locations of celestial bodies over a specific period of time—and tables of astronomical constants which are still in use.

NEWHALL Street: Henry M. Newhall, a native of Massachusetts, came to California in 1849. In San Francisco, Newhall was a leading real-estate auctioneer, and a large buyer of real estate. He founded the town which bears his name in southern California.

NEW MONTGOMERY Street: This was originally a privately constructed street, which was largely for the benefit of the Palace and Grand Hotels. It was built by William Ralston and a friend, Asbury Harpending, at their own expense in 1868–69. They had plans, which never came to fruition, to extend it from Howard Street to South Park and Rincon Hill, and from there on to the Bay. It was named after Montgomery Street and was originally called Montgomery Street South. (See Montgomery Street.)

NIAGARA Avenue: The river and world-renowned falls constitute a part of the boundary between New York state in the United States and the province of Ontario in Canada.

NIANTIC Avenue: Built about 1835, the sailing vessel *Niantic* was captained by Robert Bennett Forbes, one of the most distinguished figures in nautical America in the 19th Century. Forbes learned about the Gold Rush while in Payta, Peru, and took his whaling ship the *Niantic* to Panama. Here he loaded it with several hundred aspiring Argonauts and delivered them to San Francisco, where the ship was hauled ashore and converted into a combination office building, hotel and storeship. All the upper works burned in the great fire of May 1851. The bottom of this ship was discovered during the excavation for a highrise at the corner of Clay and Sansome streets in 1978.

NIDO Avenue: This is the Spanish word for "nest."

NIMITZ Avenue: Admiral Chester Nimitz (1885–1966) was the naval commander of the US Pacific Fleet in World War II. Nimitz is acknowledged as one of the navy's foremost administrators and strategists. He exercised authority over all land and sea forces in the Pacific theater. This is an appropriate name for a street that abuts the Hunters Point Naval Shipyard, where many navy vessels were repaired during the war.

NOB HILL Circle: See Nob Hill in the Bay Area Landmarks section.

NOE Street: José Noé was the last chief magistrate under Mexican rule, and a City official after the American occupation. Noé owned a ranch of approximately 4,000 acres in the center of present-day San Francisco. He is buried in the Mission Dolores Cemetery.

NORFOLK Street: Probably named after the hometown of one of the pioneers. There are several possible candidates. Two contenders for the honor are the Nebraskan city on the north fork of the Elkhorn River which owes its name to an abbreviation of North Fork; and Norfolk, Virginia, which is named after the English county located north of Suffolk county.

NORIEGA Street: José de la Guerra y Noriega (1792–1870) was commander of Monterey and Santa Barbara. The founder of a great family, Noriega was a city official in San Jose and fought in the Bear Flag Revolt.

NORMANDIE Terrace: The French province or district was named for the Normans, or "Northmen," the Scandinavian conquerors of this area in the 10th Century. They settled in the area that became known as the Duchy of Normandy.

NORTH POINT Street: Named after the north point which once jutted into the Bay near this street.

NORTH VIEW Court: There's a view to the north of the Bay and Alcatraz from this short street.

NORTHGATE Drive: You won't find a gate at this northern entrance to Mount Davidson manor. In the 1920s, when this subdivision was built, this name suggested exclusivity and security.

NORTHRIDGE Road: Named for its location on the north ridge of the hill that extends towards Hunters Point.

NORTHWOOD Drive: All of the street names in Westwood Park end in "wood." This is the northernmost street in this subdivision.

NORWICH Street: Probably named after the city in England. The original name for this Saxon settlement was *Northwic*.

NOTTINGHAM Place: Probably named after the town in England. The original site was occupied by the Anglo-Saxons in the Sixth Century. They bestowed on their settlement the name of *Snotingaham*—the "ham" or "village of Snot's people."

NUEVA Avenue: This is Spanish for "new."

O

O'FARRELL Street: Philadelphian Jasper O'Farrell was a civil engineer who was chosen to revise the street survey made in 1839 by Jean Jacques Vioget. The earlier survey covered the area bounded by Post, Leavenworth, and Francisco streets, and the Bay. O'Farrell corrected Vioget's street angles, which were 2½ degrees off right angles, and extended the City's streets in all directions. Some of O'Farrell's maps were reported to have caused a civic demonstration. He laid out Market Street, and the property owners protested both the diagonal mapping and the length, which at that time extended far into the country. Now motorists—as well as property owners—continue to protest the difficulties created by the diagonal swath cut by Market Street in the midst of a gridiron arrangement of other streets.

O'SHAUGHNESSY Boulevard: In 1885 Michael Maurice O'Shaughnessy arrived in San Francisco from his native Ireland at the age of 21. In the years that followed, O'Shaughnessy built dams, aqueducts, bridges, and railroads from one end of the Pacific Coast to the other, as well as in Hawaii and distant cities in the eastern United States. For 22 years, O'Shaughnessy served as San Francisco's chief engineer building tunnels, boulevards, and the municipal streetcar system. O'Shaughnessy was responsible for the Hetch Hetchy water system, which brings water to San Francisco from the Sierra Nevada.

OAK GROVE Street: There may have been an oak grove here at one time, but now all one finds above this tiny alley is the Bay Bridge freeway approach.

OAKHURST Lane: Situated in the Forest Knolls subdivision where all the street names have a "woodsy" ring, this street has yet to be developed.

OAK PARK Drive: Situated in Forest Knolls subdivision where all the streets names have a "woodsy" ring. No oaks are visible from this street, but there several bottlebrush trees may be seen.

OCEAN Avenue: Originally named Ocean House Road; this road was named for the road house that was located on this road near the Pacific Ocean.

OCTAVIA Street: Miss Octavia Gough, sister to Charles Gough, was a member of the committee that laid out and named streets in the Western Addition in 1855. (See Gough Street.)

OLD CHINATOWN Lane: The name says it all.

OLMSTEAD Street: Frederic Law Olmstead (1822–1903) was one of America's first and greatest landscape architects. He helped design Central Park in New York and the Stanford University campus in Palo Alto.

OLYMPIA Way: Named after an ancient religious sanctuary and the location of the ancient Olympic games in Greece. Since this road leads to a recreation center, it would appear to be appropriately named.

ONEIDA Avenue: The North American Indian tribe was one of the original five nations of the Iroquois League. They lived in what is now central New York.

ONONDAGA Avenue: The North American Indian tribe was one of the original five nations of the Iroquois League. In the Iroquoian tongue, their name means "on the mountain."

OPHIR Alley: Possibly named after the gold mine in Nevada, that was owned by William Ralston. (See Ralston Avenue.)

ORA Way: Mrs. Elmer (Ora) Robinson was the wife of San Francisco's thirty-third mayor, who served in office for two four-year terms starting in 1948. Her husband also had a street named for him, hence, the Robinsons are unique, since they are the only couple in San Francisco with this distinction.

ORBEN Place: In the 1970s Bert Orben, an architect, inspired this lower Pacific Heights neighborhood's redevelopment by acquiring and restoring the houses along this street. These homes were originally built in the 1880s, when the street was called Middle Street.

ORD Street: (also Court) Major General Edward Ord was commanding officer at the Presidio on two occasions in 1856. He later commanded the Department of California (1868–1871). Fort Ord, near Monterey, was also named for him.

ORIOLE Way: The passerine bird that is native to the Americas.

ORTEGA Street: José Francesco de Ortega, a Portolá expedition scout, discovered Carquinez Straits and San Francisco Bay in November 1769. Later, Ortega was commander of the Presidios of San Diego and Monterey as well as the one at Santa Barbara, which he founded. He also helped to found the missions of San Juan Capistrano and San Buenaventura.

OSAGE Alley: The North American Indian tribe of Sioux linguistic stock. The Osage migrated westward from the Atlantic Ocean to their lands in what is now Oklahoma.

OSCAR Alley: Probably named for a pioneer.

OSCEOLA Lane: Osceola Washington was a prominent community leader at Hunters Point when the Redevelopment Agency's project was planned there during the 1960s.

OTIS Street: James Otis was the twelfth mayor of San Francisco. Otis died on November 4, 1875, while serving as mayor.

OTTAWA Avenue: The territory of this Algonquian-speaking Indian tribe included what is now part of the Ottawa River, the French River, Georgian Bay, Northern Michigan, and adjacent areas.

OVERLOOK Drive: This street looks over very little other than a grove of hydrangeas in Golden Gate Park. It is no longer open to vehicular traffic.

OXFORD Street: The British town and university's name was probably derived from the district of Oxfordshire which, in turn, received its name from the River Ock that flows through the area.

PACHECO Street: A soldier in Captain Juan Anza's company in 1776, Juan Salvio Pacheco was one of the early settlers of San Francisco.

PACIFIC Avenue: The ocean was originally called *Mar del Sur* ("South Sea") by its discoverer, Vasco Nuñez de Balboa, in 1513. Its current name was given to it by Magellan some time after he passed through the Straits of Magellan in November 1570. Magellan called it *El Mar Pacifico*—possibly reflecting the transition from the turbulent waters of the Atlantic around Cape Horn to the more calm waters of the Pacific. Pacific Avenue was originally called Bartlett Street in honor of Washington Bartlett, the City's first chief judge.

PAGE Street: Robert C. Page was the clerk to the Board of Alderman from 1851 to 1856.

PAGODA Place: A pagoda is an Asian temple or sacred building with many stories that form a tower, and it would seem to be an appropriate name for one of the shortest streets in Chinatown.

PALM Avenue: Named after the Royal Palm and the other varieties of palm that grace this street.

PALO ALTO Avenue: The Spanish translation for *palo* is "stick," but in California, it colloqially means "tree," whereas *alto* is "high." Therefore, *palo alto* is "high tree." The city on the peninsula was named after Leland Stanford's farm of the same nomenclature, which was named for a tall redwood tree that stood nearby.

PALOMA Avenue: The Spanish word for "dove" or "pigeon."

PALOS Place: This Spanish word means "sticks, logs, timber, or masts," but it was used in Spanish California to denote "trees."

PALOU Avenue: Brother Francisco Palóu, a Franciscan religious official with Anza's party, took a leading role in establishing both the Presidio and Mission Dolores in 1776. Palóu had previously accompanied an exploratory expedition to this area that placed a cross on Point Lobos near Seal Rock in 1774.

PANAMA Street: The clipper ship *Panama* brought some of the Forty-Niners to San Francisco. The vessel's name was taken from the Central American country whose name means "many fish" in an Indian language. Many Forty-Niners passed through the jungles of Panama on their way to the Gold Rush.

PANORAMA Drive: This name was selected to describe the extent of the view from this street.

PARADISE Avenue: Perhaps the person who named this street believed it was not only a privilege to live in San Francisco, but also a paradise to live on this short street which now ends at the Glen Park playground.

PARAISO Place: This Spanish word means "paradise."

PARAMOUNT Terrace: In Greek/French this means "beside the mountain." This is an appropriate name for this little cul-de-sac, which is located near Lone Mountain.

PARIS Street: The French capital's name was derived from the ancient Celtic tribe called *Parisii*.

PARK Street: Probably named for the fact that this street runs to and from Holly Park.

PARK HILL Avenue: This street was named after its location, since it is adjacent to Buena Vista Park and on a hill.

PARKRIDGE Drive: An appropriate name for a street near the top of Twin Peaks, although there are more apartment houses than parkland.

PARNASSUS Avenue: This street is on the slope of Mt. Sutro and was probably named after Mount Parnassus in Greece. This mountain contains caves that were sacred to the ancient Greeks. The mythical Greek god Apollo had his sanctuary nearby.

PARROTT Alley: John Parrott came to San Francisco in 1848. He was a shipping merchant as well as a leading banker. Parrott built one of the City's first large buildings on the northwest corner of California and Montgomery streets.

PASADENA Street: The southern California city's name means "crown of the valley" in the Chippewa Indian language.

PENINSULA Avenue: The city of San Francisco is on a peninsula and this street's name is a reminder of that.

PENNSYLVANIA Avenue: The state was named for Admiral Sir William Penn (1621–1670), father of William Penn (1644–1718), by Charles II of England. Through his connections with the crown, Penn secured a large tract of land in America. He spent much of his life in America developing a colony, that was organized according to his Quaker religious beliefs and political principles. There is a double meaning to the name since, as Penn himself acknowledged, *penn* is a Welsh word meaning "head" or "headland" and, when combined with *sylvania*, a Latinized word for "woodlands," the meaning is "head woodlands" or, more clearly, "high woodlands." Since most persons are not aware of the Welsh derivation, the name is generally assumed to mean "Penn's woods." The famed Pennsylvania Avenue is in Washington, D.C.

PERALTA Avenue: Gabriel Peralta, a corporal in Anza's company, arrived in San Francisco with his four sons in 1776. When the United States took over California in 1846, the Peraltas were the owners of a 49,000-acre ranch covering what is now Berkeley, Alameda, and Oakland.

PERRY Street: Arriving in northern California in 1847, Doctor Alexander Perry was a major and a surgeon in Colonel Jonathan Stevenson's First New York Volunteer Regiment.

PERSHING Drive: General John Joseph Pershing was the commanding general of the American forces in Europe during World War I. Pershing was the first person to be appointed General of the Armies since George Washington.

PERSIA Avenue: The name of this ancient country (now Iran) originated from a region in its southern part formerly known as Persis, Pars or Parsa.

PERU Avenue: This South American country's name was derived from a Quechua Indian word implying land of abundance, a reference to the economic conditions created by the Incas who ruled the region for centuries.

PETRARCH Place: Petrarch (1304–1374) scholar, poet, and humanist—is best remembered for poems addressed to his lover, Laura. (Curiously, part of this street was once called Laura Place and today there is also a Laura Street.) These works inspired much of the Renaissance flowering of lyric poetry in Italy, France, Spain, and England.

PHELAN Avenue: A native of Ireland, James Phelan arrived in San Francisco in 1849. Phelan became a millionaire industrialist and banker. He established the First National Bank of San Francisco and was its first president. His son James D. Phelan was one of the City's most popular mayors and later became a US Senator.

PHELPS Street: A New Yorker, Timothy Guy Phelps arrived in San Francisco in 1849. He had a varied career. First, Phelps was engaged in real-estate activities, and then he was elected to the California legislature on the state's first Republican ticket in 1856. Finally, 13 years later, Phelps was appointed collector of customs for San Francisco.

PHOENIX Terrace: The mythical bird that, like San Francisco, arose reborn from the ashes. It is the City's symbol and appears on its flag and seal. Contrary to popular belief, the phoenix does not symbolize San Francisco's rebirth after the fire of 1906, but rather it commemorates the many deadly fires and subsequent rebirths of the City during the Gold Rush era.

PICO Avenue: Pio Pico served as the last Mexican governor of California in 1845–46. Los Angeles also has a Pico Street.

PIEDMONT Street: Literally, this Italian word means "foot of the mountain." It is an appropriate name for this street at the base of Mt. Olympus.

PIERCE Street: Franklin Pierce was the fourteenth President of the United States (1853–57). He acquired almost 30,000-square-miles of land from Mexico, which today comprises southern New Mexico and Arizona, to develop a southern route to California.

PILGRIM Avenue: The Pilgrims were the settlers of Plymouth, Massachusetts, the first permanent colony in New England, in 1620. They were not known as Pilgrims until two centuries later when a manuscript by William Bradford (1590–1657), a governor of Plymouth Colony, was discovered. Published in 1856, this document referred to the "saints," who had left Holland, as "pilgrimes"—from the word "pilgrimage."

PINE Street: There are at least two versions of the origin of this street's name. The first implies that it was named after a street in downtown Philadelphia by San Francisco's first civil engineer, Jean Jacques Vioget, a Swiss sailor and surveyor. The other possibility suggests that it was named for Isaac B. Pine, an early California pioneer. Pine, born in New York in 1830, arrived in San Francisco by boat in 1848. He went directly to the gold mines where, in addition to prospecting, he constructed dams, ditches, and flumes.

PINTO Avenue: Born in 1732 at Villa de Sinaloa, Pablo Pinto brought his wife and four children with him to northern California on Captain Juan Anza's expedition of 1776.

PIOCHE Street: Financier Francis Pioche is regarded as one of the City's great builders. He was a partner in the mercantile firm of Pioche and Bayerehque, which was first located on Clay Street near Portsmouth Square and later at Jackson and Montgomery streets.

PIXLEY Street: Frank Pixley was a pioneer with several careers. He was one of the first editors of *The Argonaut*, a well-known San Francisco newspaper. Pixley, a prominent Republican, was elected city attorney in 1850 and eight years later, he was elected to the State Assembly. In 1869, President Grant appointed him California's district attorney.

PIZARRO Way: Probably named after Francisco Pizarro (1457–1541), who was with Balboa when he discovered the Pacific Ocean. Pizarro helped conquer the Inca Empire of Peru; he consolidated Spanish power there and founded Lima.

THE PLAZA and Plaza Street: This Spanish word colloquially means "village square," where the heart of a town or its center of activity is usually located. Not descriptive of these particular streets, which are found in a residential area. The Plaza is located in St. Francis Woods, while Plaza Street is located across from the Laguna Honda Hospital. The developers of these two streets may have thought that this name would give an air of distinction to their respective projects.

PLEASANT Street: Mary Ellen (Mammy) Pleasant (1814?–1904), an African-American who came to San Francisco in about 1849, ran a boarding and bawdy house and used her money to aid runaway slaves and other struggling blacks. Later, she became the housekeeper for a local banker, Thomas Bell, whom she apparently dominated. A small park on what was Bell's property, at the southwest corner of Bush and Octavia streets is named for her. The story *Mammy Pleasant*, by Helen Holdredge, was written about her.

PLYMOUTH Avenue: Probably named after the city in Massachusetts, the site of the first permanent settlement by Europeans in New England. It was named for the city in England from which these settlers, the Puritans, departed. In turn, this town's name was derived from the fact that it was situated at the mouth of the Plym River estuary.

POINT LOBOS Avenue: The Spanish word, *lobos* means "wolves," but along the California coast the word has been applied to seals and sea lions. This street is so named because it goes to and from Point Lobos, a spot close to Seal Rock, where sea lions often sunbathe.

POLARIS Way: Located on the slope of San Bruno Mountain, this street is named after the North Star at the end of the Little Dipper.

POLK Street: James K. Polk was the eleventh President of the United States (1845–49). Under his leadership, the United States acquired vast territories along the Pacific Coast and in the Southwest. Today, this land is divided into Texas, New Mexico, Oregon, and California. In his last message to Congress, he gave the official imprimatur to the wild, but true, tales of gold in California.

POMONA Street: Probably named for the southern California city that was named after the Roman goddess of fruit and fruit trees.

POND Street: Edward B. Pond was a two-term mayor of San Francisco from 1887 to 1890. The head of a wholesale firm, he moved to San Francisco from Chico, California. He was elected to the Board of Supervisors in 1882 and served two terms before running for mayor.

PONTIAC Alley: Probably named after the Ottawa Indian Chief who became one of America's greatest intertribal leaders. He organized the resistance by several tribes to the British takeover in the Great Lakes area after the British victory in the French and Indian War (1754–63).

POPE Street: Major General John Pope was the commander of the military district of the Pacific and the Department of California from 1883 to 1886. Pope was in charge of the survey for the route of the Central Pacific Railway.

PORTOLA Street: (also Drive) Gaspar de Portolá was the first Spanish governor of California. In 1769, Portolá marched north from San Diego in command of the first party of Europeans to see San Francisco Bay. Portola Street is located in the Presidio. Portola Drive begins where Upper Market Street ends and offers a spectacular view of the City and the Bay.

POST Street: Merchant Gabriel B. Post came to San Francisco in 1847 and was one of the City's early civic leaders. In 1849, Post became a member of the Town Council. Later, he was elected to the state Senate.

POTRERO Street: This is the Spanish word for "pasture" or "cattle ground." The street runs through an area that was a pasture in San Francisco's early days.

POWELL Street: Doctor William J. Powell was a surgeon on the U.S. war sloop, *Warren*, which brought him to San Francisco. In 1847, Charles Lyman, a surveyor working on the mapping of San Francisco, lived in the same house as Powell, who by then had established a "sanitorium" for sick sailors. Undoubtedly, Lyman suggested that this street be named for Powell.

POWHATTAN Avenue: A powerful Indian chief, Powhattan, was the father of Pocahontas. He was the founder and leader of a confederacy of at least 30 Algonquian-speaking Indian tribes who occupied most of what is now tidewater Virginia, the eastern shore of the Chesapeake Bay, and possibly southern Maryland.

PRADO Street: In Spanish, this word means "meadow."

PRAGUE Street: The capital of the Czech Republic is that nation's leading cultural and economic center.

PRECITA Avenue: Named after the adjacent park of the same name whose name in Spanish means "condemned to Hell."

PRENTISS Street: Possibly named for Benjamin M. Prentiss, a Union general during the Civil War. He commanded the Sixth Division Army of the Tennessee at Shiloh, where he was captured. After his release, he commanded the East Military District in Arkansas. After the war, Prentiss practiced law.

PRESIDIO Avenue: (also Boulevard and Terrace) This Spanish word means "garrison" or "fortified barracks." These streets were named for the fact that they lead to, through, or are near the Presidio, the military installation founded by the Spanish in 1776.

PRINCETON Street: Named after the University in New Jersey which took its name from the borough and township in which it is situated. Originally named Stoney Brook, in 1724 the town was renamed to honor William III, Prince of Orange-Nassau. This is one of a series of streets in this part of the City—the Excelsior District—that was named for a college or university by the land developers, the University Homestead Association in the 1860s.

PUEBLO Street: This is the Spanish word for "town" or "people."

PUTNAM Street: Named for either Arthur Putnam, a famous San Francisco sculptor, who lived in Bernal Heights around the 1860s or, more probably, for the Revolutionary War general Israel Putnam (1718–1790), who fought in the Battles of Lexington, Concord, and Bunker Hill. He is also known for his unsuccessful attempt to capture Havana in 1762.

QUARRY Road: This road passes through an old quarry in the Presidio.

QUESADA Avenue: Gonzalo Jiminez de Quesada (1499–1579) was one of the greatest Spanish conquerors of New Granada—the Spanish holdings in South America in the early 16th Century. Since he spent 34 years unsuccessfully seeking El Dorado, a legendary land abundant in gold and other precious metals, some persons think he was Cervantes' model for Don Quixote.

QUICKSTEP Lane: Since the *Quickstep* was a three-masted barkentine, this is an appropriate name for a street in a housing project sponsored by the International Longshoremen's Union. Built in 1884 by S.B. Peterson, she was put afloat in 1900, but abandoned at sea on November 24, 1904.

QUINCY Street: Probably named after the city in Massachusetts, which was named in honor of John Quincy, a prominent local resident. John Quincy Adams and his father, John Adams, both presidents of the United States, were born and are buried there.

QUINT Street: A native of New Hampshire, Leander Quint came to California in 1849 with a law degree. After working in the mines, Quint opened a law practice in Sonora. He was later elected a judge in Tuolumne County. Quint came to San Francisco in 1865, where he practiced law until his death in 1890.

QUINTARA Street: This name was probably selected by the Parkside Realty Company—which developed this part of the Sunset district around the turn of the 20th Century—because the developers liked the way the name sounded. Most of the streets in this portion of the City are named after members of Captain Juan Anza's expedition to northern California in 1776, but there was no one in the expedition whose name began with the letter "Q," so this name was undoubtedly selected at random.

RACCOON Drive: Probably named after the English 16-gun war sloop *Raccoon* which scraped bottom off the northern California coast in 1814 and limped into the Bay for repairs. The vessel was named after the familiar animal with short legs, pointed nose, small erect ears and a bushy tail.

RACINE Lane: Probably named after the city and county in Wisconsin whose name is French for "root."

RALEIGH Street: Probably named after Sir Walter Raleigh (1554–1617), an English adventurer, a favorite of Queen Elizabeth I, and an unsuccessful early American colonist.

RALSTON Avenue: (Also Street) William Chapman Ralston was born in Plymouth, Ohio, in 1826. As a young man, Ralston sailed to San Francisco by way of Panama. He was one of the City's foremost bankers, industrialists, and civic leaders. Ralston built the Palace Hotel and founded the Bank of California with Darius Ogden Mills. He died in a drowning accident at the age of 49. His biography is entitled *The Man Who Built San Francisco*—only a slight exaggeration.

RANKIN Street: Ira P. Rankin was a well-known pioneer. Born in Hampshire County, Massachusetts, in 1817, Rankin left for San Francisco by way of Panama in May 1852. After success as a merchant, he went into the foundry business. President Lincoln appointed Rankin as collector of the port. Rankin ran unsuccessfully for Congress but held a number of civic positions such as president of the Chamber of Commerce, president of the Mercantile Library, and trustee of Lick College and the College of California.

RAUSCH Street: Joseph N. Rausch was a Forty-Niner about whom not much else is known.

RAVENWOOD Drive: One of a series of streets in Westwood Highlands which have the same suffix.

RAYCLIFF Terrace: Perched on a cliff in Pacific Heights this street was named for Milton S. Ray, founder of the Ray Burner Company. Ray was also an ornithologist and poet. He was a curator and director of the Pacific Museum of Ornithology, and he lived near where this street runs into Pacific Avenue.

RED ROCK Way: Named after the hill around which this street winds.

REDONDO Street: This is the Spanish word for "round."

REED Street: Reed was one of the survivors of the Donner party, a group of immigrants who unsuccessfully tried to cross the Sierra Nevada in the winter of 1846–47. The Donner party is famous because deep snow stalled the group, forcing some members to resort to cannibalism.

REGENT Street: Possibly named after the street of the same name in London.

RENO Place: Probably named after the city in Nevada, which describes itself as "the biggest little city in the west." Reno is situated near the base of the eastern slope of the Sierra Nevada. Reno was named for General Jessie Lee Reno of Virginia, a Union officer who was killed in the Civil War.

REPOSA Way: A Spanish word, *reposa* means "rest."

RESERVOIR Street: There was a reservoir on this site until the mid-1860s. It belonged to the San Francisco Water Company which was absorbed by the Spring Valley Water Company in 1864.

RETIRO Way: A Spanish word, *retiro* means "retreat."

REUEL Court: Reuel Brady was a prominent community leader in Hunters Point during the 1960s when the Redevelopment Agency's project there was under construction.

REVERE Avenue: Paul Revere is a folk hero of the American Revolution. His dramatic horseback ride on the night of April 18, 1775, warning Boston area residents that the British were coming, was immortalized in a poem by Henry Wadsworth Longfellow.

REX Avenue: This is the Latin word for "king."

REY Avenue: Jacques J. Rey was a lithographer in San Francisco in the 1860s and 1870s.

RHINE Street: This major waterway of the European continent flows west, north and then northwest from the Alps for 820 miles, passing through six countries before it empties into the North Sea.

RHODE ISLAND Street: The origin of this state's name is uncertain—there are two rival theories. The first version is that an island (now called Aquidneck Island and part of the state) may have been the one sighted by the Italian explorer Giovanni di Verrazao in 1524. He said it was about the size of the island of Rhodes in the Dodecanese Islands off the west coast of Asia Minor. The other possibility is that the island was seen by the Dutch explorer Adraien Block who named it *Roodt Eylandt*, "red island." In any event, early English settlers used the Indian name, Aquidneck Island, until 1644 when it was changed to the "Isle of Rhodes." Later, the colony was called "Rhode Island and the Providence Plantations."

RICHARD HENRY DANA Place: This famous writer is associated with early San Francisco's history. He first arrived in 1835 at the age of 25 when the City was in its infancy. His popular book, *Two Years Before the Mast*, described his voyage around the Cape to California. It was published in 1840, after his return to Boston to practice maritime law.

RICHARDSON Avenue: William A. Richardson was one of the first inhabitants of Yerba Buena (now San Francisco) in 1835. He drew the first map of the town. Later, Richardson became captain of the port and bought a large ranch, which is now Sausalito. Richardson Bay, near Sausalito, was also named for him.

RICO Way: Rico is the Spanish word for "rich."

RILEY Avenue: Brigadier General Bennet Riley was a native of Maryland who became military governor of California in 1849. Lacking congressional authority for governing the newly-acquired territory, Riley issued a proclamation calling for the election of delegates to a state convention, which drafted a constitution for what became the State of California.

RINCON Street: This Spanish word means "corner." The southern point of Yerba Buena harbor was originally called Rincon Point. The former harbor has been filled in with land and now supports the western approaches to the Bay Bridge.

RINGGOLD Street: Lieutenant Cawalader Ringgold was a member of the first US expedition in the Pacific in 1841. Ringgold commanded the USS *Porpoise* and led a survey mapping the Sacramento River as far west as Colusa; he also surveyed parts of San Francisco Bay.

RIO Court: This is the Spanish word for "river."

RIO VERDE Street: This is Spanish for "green river."

RIVAS Avenue: Maria Gertrudis Rivas, the wife of Ignacio Linares, a veteran soldier in Captain Juan Anza's party, came to San Francisco in 1776. She accompanied her husband and brought their four children.

RIVERA Street: See Moncada Street.

RIVOLI Street: Probably named after the street of the same name in Paris.

RIZAL Street: José Rizal y Mercado (1861–1896), "The father of the Philippines," was a physician and a man of letters. His life and literary works were an inspiration to the Philippine nationalist movement.

ROACH Street: Phillip Roach was a pioneer, politician, and public administrator. In 1845, President Polk appointed Roach consul in Lisbon, Portugal, but instead Roach opted to come to California. He initially lived in Monterey, where he first became a magistrate, then that city's first mayor, and in 1853, a State Senator. Subsequently, he moved to San Francisco where he became the appraiser of the port, and he was elected twice as the City's public administrator.

ROANOKE Street: Probably named after the city in Virginia or the river which flows from southwest Virginia to Albemarle Sound, North Carolina. Another possible origin for the name is the island on which was born the first child of English parents in the New World (Virginia Dare, August 18, 1587). In any event, this word is the Indian term for shells that were used as money.

ROBERT KIRK Lane: Named after the clothing store founded by Robert Kirk which was once located next to this alley.

ROBIN HOOD Drive: The famed English rebel of Sherwood Forest was the hero of a series of English ballads, some of which date from the 14th Century. Many of the most striking episodes in the tales describe him and his companions as robbing and killing wealthy representatives of authority and giving the spoils to the poor. The street is located in a subdivision known as Sherwood Forest.

ROBINSON Drive: Elmer Robinson was San Francisco's thirty-third mayor from 1948 to 1956. A native San Franciscan, Robinson was admitted to the State Bar in 1915. Before running for mayor, Robinson was appointed to the Municipal Court where he became a Superior Court judge. A Republican, he was responsible for the City's first attempt at urban renewal. His wife, Ora, also had a street named for her. The

Robinsons are unique, since they are the only San Francisco couple with this distinction. This street is next to a street named for the thirty-second mayor of San Francisco, Roger Lapham.

ROCKIDGE Drive: There are no "rocks" on this street situated at the top of Golden Gate Heights and adjacent to Cragmont Avenue.

ROLPH Street: James Rolph, Jr. served as mayor of San Francisco for 19 consecutive years (1911–1930) before becoming Governor of California in 1931. He died in office three years later. During "Sunny Jim's" mayoral term, San Francisco emerged as a modern city. When he took office, the City was still recovering from the effects of the 1906 fire and earthquake. By the time he left office, the Civic Center had been planned and the City Hall and auditorium had been completed.

ROME Street: According to a Roman fable, Romulus and Remus, twin sons of the god Mars, were abandoned on the flooding Tiber River and then deposited by the receding waters at the foot of the Palantine, one of the major hills of present day Rome, Italy's capital city. Suckled by a shewolf, these boys were reared by a shepherd and grew up to found Rome—to which Romulus gave his name.

ROOSEVELT Way: Since this street acquired its name in the mid-1920s, it was probably named for Theodore Roosevelt, the twenty-sixth President of the United States. He was also a writer, explorer, and soldier. He was elected Vice President in 1900 and succeeded McKinley when he was assassinated the following year. Roosevelt was reelected in his own right in 1904. He ran again for the presidency in 1912 on the Progressive party's ticket, but he was defeated.

ROSEWOOD Drive: One of a number of streets in Westwood Highlands with the suffix of "wood."

ROSIE LEE Lane: Rosie Lee Williams was a prominent community leader in Hunters Point during the 1960s when the Redevelopment Agency's project there was under construction.

ROSS Alley: Merchant Charles L. Ross was an alderman in the early 1850s.

ROSSI Avenue: Angelo Rossi was mayor of San Francisco for 14 years starting in 1930. During his tenure, the Civic Center was completed, and the tax rate was reduced to its lowest level in 25 years.

ROUSSEAU Street: The De Boom family owned the tract of land on which this street is found. They named it for a Belgian friend who was the father of Charles and Oliver Rousseau of yachting fame.

RUCKMAN Avenue: Named in 1923 to honor Major General John W. Ruckman, the commanding officer of Fort Baker from February 1909 until November 1910.

RUSS Street: Imanuel Charles Christian Russ arrived in San Francisco with his family in March 1847. A jeweler in New York, upon his arrival in San Francisco, Russ opened a jewelry store. During the Gold Rush, the store became an assay office. His family built a hotel on Montgomery street between Pine and Bush streets near the site where the Russ building is currently. The purchase price of the land for the hotel was for less than $50—about the cost of what a square inch would be today at the same location.

RUSSIA Avenue: The country's name is derived from the *Rus*, a nomadic tribe of Eastern Slavs who roamed the Upper Volga River area in the Ninth Century.

RUSSIAN HILL Place: See Russian Hill in the Bay Area Landmarks section of this book.

RUTLAND Street: Possibly named after either a town in England or the Earls and Dukes of Rutland—English titles held by members of the Manners family since 1525.

SABIN Place: As president of the Pacific States Telephone and Telegraph, John Sabin was considered to be the "Father of the Pacific Coast telephone system." In 1847, he started his communications career as a messenger boy in New York City for Western Union. He helped to establish a telegraph line across the Bering Straits to Siberia and then through Russia to Europe. In San Francisco Sabin organized the first telephone company on the Pacific Coast.

SACRAMENTO Street: Situated in the Central Valley where the American and Sacramento rivers meet, the capital of California was named for the Sacramento River. Originally called Rio de San Francisco, the name of the river was changed to Sacramento, which is Spanish for the Holy Sacrament. Sacramento Street was originally called Howard Street in honor of William Howard, a member of the first City Council.

SAINT CHARLES Avenue: Possibly named after the well-known street of the same name in New Orleans.

SAINT ELMO Way: The name St. Elmo is an Italian corruption of St. Erasmus, the patron saint of Mediterranean sailors.

SAINT FRANCIS Boulevard: This street is a wide, main thoroughfare leading into the exclusive neighborhood of St. Francis Wood. This 175-acre development was named after St. Francis of Assisi, for whom San Francisco was named.

SAINT GERMAIN Avenue: There are at least two important Sts. Germain. The first is St. Germain of Auxerre (378–448), an important Gallic prelate twice sent on crucial missions from Rome to England to help consolidate the British church. The other is St. Germain of Paris (496–576), an abbot and bishop, who was one of France's most revered saints and an important, though unsuccessful, mediator in the fratricidal civil war among several Merovingian Kings.

SAINT JOSEPH'S Avenue: St. Joseph was the husband of the Virgin Mary. This street received its name because it was situated next to the Calvary Catholic cemetery.

SAINT LOUIS Alley: Probably named after St. Louis (1274–1297), who was the greatnephew of St. Louis, King of France. The former was confined in Barcelona for seven years as a hostage in exchange for his father, a prisoner of war. Upon his release, St. Louis joined the Franciscan Order and was appointed Bishop of Toulouse.

SAINT MARY'S Avenue: Named for St. Mary's College, once located nearby.

SALINAS Avenue: *Salina*, a Spanish word, means "salt-pit." Both the river and county seat were named for the salt marshes and ponds near the river's mouth.

SALMON Street: Named after the fish.

SAMOSET Street: He was a 17th Century Pemaquid Indian who befriended the Puritans after they landed in Massachusetts.

SAN ANDREAS Way: San Andreas was the name of an early rancho in the Santa Cruz area. Andreas, or Andrew, was one of the Apostles. He was the elder brother of St. Peter and a disciple of John the Baptist. Tradition has it that he was crucified in Greece during the reign of Nero.

SAN ANSELMO Avenue: San Anselmo was the name of an early, large ranch. It was situated in Marin County where the town and adjacent valley of San Anselmo are found. The ranch was probably named for St. Anselm (1033–1109).

SAN ANTONIO Place: Probably named after St. Anthony of Padua, patron saint of the Franciscan Order. He joined the Franciscans in 1221, and died at Padua in 1231. He was noted as a preacher and a worker of miracles.

SAN BENITO Way: The street name comes from an early rancho in Monterey County, which was named for St. Benedict, founder of the Benedictine Order. This is one of many streets starting with "San" in the exclusive St. Francis Wood neighborhood.

SAN BUENAVENTURA Way: In 1782, this Mission was founded in Ventura. It was named to honor St. Bonaventure, a Franciscan saint in the 13th Century.

SAN CARLOS Street: On August 5, 1775, Captain Juan Manuel Ayala, commanding the *San Carlos*, sailed through the Golden Gate and anchored off what is now called Angel Island. One year later the same boat returned carrying the tools and supplies needed to construct the Presidio. It is probable that the street was named for this ship. There was also a mission founded in 1770 in Monterey called Mission San Carlos Borromeo which was named after a 16th Century Archbishop of Milan and it is now called San Carlos Cathedral, the royal Presidio chapel.

SAN DIEGO Avenue: In 1769, Mission San Diego de Alcalá was founded in the area that is now San Diego. It was the first mission in California, and it was named to honor San Diego de Alcalá, a Franciscan saint in the 15th Century.

SAN FELIPE Avenue: The street name came from an early, large rancho, which was named after one of the several Sts. Phillip. The ranch was located near Mission San Juan Bautista. This is one of the many streets starting with "San" in the exclusive St. Francis Woods subdivision.

SAN FERNANDO Way: In 1797, Mission San Fernando Rey de España was founded in San Fernando. This mission was named to honor St. Ferdinand III, King of Leon and Castile.

SAN GABRIEL Avenue: In 1771, Mission San Gabriel Archangel, was founded in San Gabriel, an area just east of Los Angeles. The mission was named to honor the Archangel Gabriel, "the angel of the Incarnation and of Consolation and of the Power of God."

SAN JACINTO Way: This street name comes from an early, large California ranch probably named after St. Hyacinth of Silesia. The Spanish word *jacinto* means "hyacinth."

SAN JOSE Avenue: Mission San Jose was founded near San Jose in 1797. This city was named for St. Joseph, the husband of the Virgin Mary.

SAN JUAN Avenue: In 1797, the Mission San Juan Bautista was founded in the town of San Juan Bautista near Hollister. In English, the name of the mission is "St. John, the Baptist."

SAN LEANDRO Way: The street name comes from an early, large ranch that was located in the vicinity of the present East Bay community of San Leandro. It was probably named after St. Leander, Archbishop of Seville.

SAN LORENZO Way: The street name comes from an early Alameda County rancho, which was probably named after St. Lawrence of Rome who was roasted to death by Emperor Valerian in 258 A.D.

SAN LUIS Avenue: Mission San Luis Obispo de Tolosa (St. Louis, bishop of Toulouse) was established in 1772 by Father Junípero Serra. St. Louis (1274–1297) was the great nephew of St. Louis, King of France.

SAN MARCOS Avenue: The street name comes from Mark, the Apostle, who is traditionally thought to be the author of the second Gospel of the New Testament.

SAN MATEO Avenue: The street name comes from the Mission hospice which was built in this west bay community in 1793. This name was derived from a nearby dry river bed which was named by Captain Juan Anza in 1776 to honor Matthew, the evangelist, apostle, and legendary author of one of the four Gospels.

SAN MIGUEL Street: An early Mexican land grant, Rancho San Miguel once occupied the Outer Mission area where this street is located. This ranch may have been named after Mission San Miguel Archangel which was founded in 1797 in San Miguel, California. Both the mission and town were named for the Archangel Michael.

SAN PABLO Avenue: Named after an early rancho located in what is now Contra Costa County. The ranch was named for Paul, the apostle.

SAN RAFAEL Way: In 1817, Mission San Rafael Archangel was founded in San Rafael, which is now the county seat of Marin. St. Raphael the Archangel was one of three such angels venerated by the Catholic Church. The other two archangels were Michael and Gabriel. (See the entry for San Rafael in the Bay Area landmarks section for additional information.)

SAN RAMON Way: The street was named after an early, large ranch, which was probably named for St. Raymond, a Roman martyr. This ranch was located in what is now known as Contra Costa County near the town of Danville.

SANCHEZ Street: A son of one of Captain Juan Anza's soldiers and a famous Indian fighter, José Antonio Sánchez was a commander of the Presidio. His family acquired extensive land holdings south of present-day South San Francisco. Sánchez is buried in the cemetery at Mission Dolores.

SANSOME Street: Named after Sansome Street in downtown Philadelphia by Jean Jacques Vioget, a Swiss sailor, surveyor, and the City's first municipal engineer. There is also reason to suspect that George Hyde, a City official (and a native of Philadelphia) also proposed this street's name in 1847. Philadelphia's Sansom Street (without the "e") was named for William Sansom, a home builder who conceived the concept of row houses in 1803.

SANTA ANA Avenue: The street was named after an early, large California ranch, which was named after St. Anne, the mother of the Virgin Mary.

SANTA BARBARA Avenue: In 1786, the mission was established in Santa Barbara. The city of Santa Barbara was named by Sebastian Vizcaino in 1602 to honor the patron saint of Mariners.

SANTA CLARA Avenue: In 1777, Mission Santa Clara de Asis was founded in Santa Clara. St. Clare of Assisi was the co-founder of the Franciscan Order of Poor Clares. She was the first woman to embrace the Franciscan Order in the 13th Century.

SANTA CRUZ Avenue: In 1791, the mission was established in Santa Cruz. This is the Spanish for "Holy Cross."

SANTA MONICA Way: The street was named for an early, large California ranch with the same name. St. Monica was the mother of St. Augustine.

SANTA PAULA Avenue: The street was named after an early, large California ranch with the same name. St. Paula was a noble Roman matron who became a disciple of Saint Jerome.

SANTA RITA Avenue: The street was named after an early Alameda County rancho. St. Rita de Casis was a part of the Augustinian order.

SANTA YNEZ Avenue: In 1804, Santa Ynez (St. Ines) Mission was founded in Solvang. St. Ines was named to honor St. Agnes of Assisi who lived in the 13th Century. She was a sister of St. Clare and one of the first to embrace the religious life under the rule of St. Francis as a Poor Clare or Minoress.

SANTA YSABEL Avenue: This street was named after an early, large ranch which was probably named in honor of St. Elizabeth of Portugal, daughter of the King of Aragon.

SANTIAGO Street: Probably named for the *Santiago*, a sailing ship which visited San Diego and Monterey hauling provisions and personnel for Captain Juan Anza's expedition of 1776. The street was named by the Parkside Realty Company, the developers of this outer Sunset area around the turn of the 20th Century.

SANTOS Street: In Spanish and Portuguese this word means "saints."

SATURN Street: The god of sowing or seed in Roman mythology.

SAWYER Street: Henry Schwerin, the developer of Visitacion Valley Homestead, named this neighborhood street after a friend in 1868.

SCENIC Way: An appropriate name for a street that has a beautiful view of the Golden Gate.

SCHWERIN Street: Henry Schwerin, a native of Germany, arrived in San Francisco in January 1850. One year later he established a bakery business, and after marrying Ottilia—for whom a street is named in Daly City—he moved to a 300-acre parcel in Visitacion Valley, which he subdivided in April 1868. His son Ted married Kate McCarthy whose father, Peter, is reputed to have been the namesake of a street in Visitacion Valley.

SCOTIA Avenue: The name originated in the 11th Century when the southwestern part of what is now Scotland, was settled by a tribe of Scots who migrated there from Ireland.

SCOTLAND Street: The country was originally known as Caledonia. The current name originated from a group of Scots who migrated to this area in the 11th Century.

SCOTT Street: General Winfield Scott was a US General during three wars. (Scott participated in the War of 1812 and in the Mexican War, and he commanded the US Army at the outbreak of the Civil War.) He has the distinction of commanding the US Army longer than any other individual, from 1841 to 1861. In 1852 he was the unsuccessful Whig candidate for President. A post within the Presidio is named for him. He is probably one of only three individuals whose first and last names or whose double last names are used separately to name two different streets in San Francisco. The other street that is probably named for Scott is Winfield Street, and the two other persons are Captain Fernando Rivera y Moncada and Mark Aldrich. (See Winfield Street.)

SEA CLIFF Avenue: The street takes its name from the exclusive residential district of northwestern San Francisco which derives its name from the fact that it is perched on a cliff overlooking the sea.

SEA VIEW Terrace: As the name implies, there is a good view of the ocean from this street, which is located in the northwest corner of the City.

SEAL ROCK Drive: Named for nearby Seal Rock, where the sea lions live and play off the coast at Ocean Beach in front of the Cliff House.

SECURITY PACIFIC Place: This alley was formerly Savings Union Place. The name was changed when Security Pacific, now defunct, occupied a building along this street.

SELBY Street: A New York merchant, Thomas H. Selby came to San Francisco in 1849 hoping to earn enough to pay his creditors after his business in the East had failed. He was successful as a metal importer and in 1851, was elected a member of the Board of Aldermen where he led an effort to reorganize the Police Department. In 1869, he was elected to a four-year term as mayor by only 110 votes. Selby also founded the Selby Smelting Company and built the Selby Shot Tower.

SEMINOLE Avenue:. The name Seminole has been given various meanings, among them "runaway" and "pioneer." The word may have been derived from the Spanish *cimarron* which means "wild." This Indian tribe now resides in Florida.

SENECA Avenue: This Iroquois-speaking tribe lived in what is now western New York State and eastern Ohio. They were the largest, and one of the most important, of the original five nations of the Iroquois League.

SERGEANT JOHN V. YOUNG Street: A police officer who was killed while on duty at the Ingleside police station in 1971. The station is located on this street in Balboa Park.

SERRANO Drive: In 1776, Ana Regina Serrano accompanied Captain Juan Anza's expedition to northern California.

SEVILLE Street: The city in southern Spain is important in history as a cultural center, a capital of Muslim Spain, and a center for Spanish exploration of the New World.

SEWARD Street: Probably named for the Secretary of State who served under both Abraham Lincoln and Andrew Johnson. He conducted the negotiations with Russia to purchase Alaska in 1867. Alaska was known as "Seward's Folly," since the price of 7.2-million dollars was considered outrageous at that time.

SHAFTER Avenue: (Also Road) Named in 1939 to honor General William R. Shafter, commander of the United States Army in Cuba. General Shafter received the Medal of Honor for his bravery in the Civil War. He also was commanding officer of the Department of California from May 1877 to 1898, and again from 1899 to 1901.

SHAKESPEARE Street: The British playwright and poet, is widely regarded as the greatest English-language writer of all time. His plays, written in the late 16th and early 17th centuries for a small repertory theatre, are now performed more often and in more countries than ever. As Ben Jonson said, "Shakespeare was not of an age, but for all time."

SHARON Street: Lawyer William Sharon came west from the state of Mississippi in 1849. He was a realtor, banker, miner, and a US Senator. His donation was instrumental in building Golden Gate Park's Children's Playground, the first such facility in the United States. Sharon was regarded as a crafty and sometimes shady manipulator of men and money.

SHAWNEE Avenue: The Algonquian-speaking North American Indian tribe, whose first known home was the central Ohio River Valley, now reside in Oklahoma.

SHELLEY Drive: John F. Shelley, the thirty-fifth mayor of San Francisco (1964–1968), was born in the South Park district in 1905. At 32, he became president of the San Francisco Labor Council. He was a US Congressman prior to assuming the City's highest office. He experienced a turbulent term as mayor, prompting one observer to note that he was the City's "unluckiest mayor."

SHERMAN Street: (also Road) Lieutenant General William Tecumseh Sherman was an American Civil War general, who is considered an important theoretician of modern warfare. Prior to his participation in the Civil War, Sherman ran the Bank of Lucas Turner in San Francisco. Sherman led the Union forces in crushing campaigns through the South. He is often quoted as saying "War is Hell."

SHERWOOD Court: Located half a block from Robin Hood Drive, this street may have been named for Sherwood Forest in England, a haunt of this legendary outlaw. Most of the streets in Westwood Highlands— where this street is located—have the suffix "wood."

SHORE VIEW Terrace: There is a view of the south shore of Marin County from this street.

SHORT Street: Although by no means the shortest street in San Francisco, the name may still be derived from the fact that this street is only one block long.

SHOTWELL Street: J. M. Shotwell was the secretary of the Merchant's Exchange and a cashier in Alsop and Company's bank.

SHRADER Street: A. I. Shrader, a member of the Board of Supervisors from the Ninth Ward from 1865 to 1872, was instrumental in the creation of Golden Gate Park.

SIERRA Street: This California county was named after the Spanish word for "mountain range." *Sierra Nevada* means the "snowy mountain range" or the "sierra white as snow."

SILVER Avenue: This was a pioneer family with large property interests in San Francisco and Monterey counties.

SIMONDS Loop: Named to honor Major General George S. Simonds in 1940. Simonds was acting Chief of Staff of the US Army from 1927 until 1931, and deputy Chief of Staff from 1935 to 1936. He died at Letterman General Hospital in the Presidio.

SKYLINE Boulevard: While there is no view of San Francisco's downtown skyline from this street, there is an excellent view of San Francisco's hills (Twin Peaks, Mt. Davidson, and Mt. Sutro).

SKYVIEW Way: Most of the streets in this residential subdivision, Midtown Terrace, which is nestled near the top of Twin Peaks, have "view" for a suffix.

SLOAT Boulevard: Commodore John Drake Sloat took command of the US Navy squadron in the Pacific in 1846. Sloat captured Monterey on July 7, 1846, and two days later, Montgomery landed and seized Yerba Buena from the Mexicans. Yerba Buena was renamed San Francisco shortly thereafter.

SOLA Avenue: Pablo Vicente de Sola was the tenth governor of Mexican California (1815–1823) and the last under Spanish rule. Sola was originally a soldier, who came with Captain Juan Anza when he established a settlement in San Francisco in 1776.

SOMERSET Street: Probably named after the town in southwestern England.

SONOMA Street: Probably named after the county located north of San Francisco and Marin. This county was named for the Wintun Indian word for "nose," referring to the land or tribe of "Chief Nose."

SOTELO Avenue: A member of Captain Juan Anza's expedition to northern California in 1776, Sotelo was one of the first settlers in San Francisco.

SOUTH HILL Boulevard: This street goes up (and down) South Hill which originally got its name because it's located in the southern part of San Francisco.

SOUTH PARK Avenue: South Park was created in 1854 by Englishman George Gordon in an attempt to recreate a typical residential block of London. For several years, it was a very stylish address. The street runs parallel to, and takes its name from, the park which was located south of, what was at the time, the prevailing center of town.

SOUTH VAN NESS Avenue: This street was originally part of Howard Street, but it had such an unsavory reputation that the residents of the lower part of Howard Street did not want to be associated with it. Consequently, they opted for the present name for their part. (See Van Ness Avenue for the origin of the name.)

SOUTHERN HEIGHTS Avenue: This street is located on the slope of Potrero Hill, which at the time of its construction, was in the southern part of town.

SOUTHWOOD Drive: The southernmost of all the streets in Westwood Park, where all thoroughfares have the suffix "wood."

SPARROW Street: This tiny alley in the Lower Mission District was informally named a number of years ago by the neighborhood boys for their nemesis "Old Man Sparrow," and later the name was made official by the Board of Supervisors. Who exactly was "Old Man Sparrow" is lost to history.

SPARTA Street: The Greek town that is famed for its military oligarchy, emerged as the most powerful city-state in Greece, when it defeated Athens in the Peloponnesian War of 404 B.C.

SPEAR Street: This street was probably named for Nathan Spear, an early immigrant to California. In 1836 he moved to Yerba Buena where he and two partners operated a store and trading post. He helped erect the first frame house in San Francisco that same year. Three years later, he built the first flour mill in California. Although less likely, it is also possible that this street might have been named after Forty-Niner Willis Bradford Spear, an army scout with General Winfield Scott in Mexico. He bought the first lot, which was underwater at the time, on what is now Spear Street.

SPRINGFIELD Drive: Possibly named after the town in Massachusetts (or Illinois or Ohio or New Jersey or Vermont), all of which were named after a town in England. There are only a handful of states which do not have a town called Springfield.

SPROUL Lane: Willliam Sproul started working for the Southern Pacific Railroad in 1882, and he rose through the ranks to become its president in 1911. He built a large mansion at the intersection of Yerba Buena Lane and Sacramento Street. After Sproul's death, his widow prevailed upon the city to have the name of the Yerba Buena Lane changed in his honor.

STANFORD Street: Leland Stanford (1824–1893) who started out as a grocer, became governor of California, a member of the United States Senate, a railroad builder, and founder of one of the most prestigious universities in America. He was a member of the "Big Four"—the owners of the Central Pacific Railroad.

STANFORD HEIGHTS Avenue: See above.

STANLEY Street: Ira Stanley was a Forty-Niner.

STANTON Street: Perhaps the last street in the city to be paved. Who the street was named for is unknown.

STANYAN Street: (also Boulevard) C. H. Stanyan was a City Supervisor and a member of the Commission to Appraise Outside Lands in 1872. The outside lands were all the countryside west of Divisadero Street. Stanyan fought unsuccessfully to have the Golden Gate Park Panhandle extended as a parkway all the way to Market Street.

STARR KING Way: Born in New York in 1824, Rev. Thomas Starr King was the spiritual leader of San Francisco's First Unitarian Church. At 21, he was ordained in the ministry; two years later he was asked to come to San Francisco. He soon began making passionate pro-Union speeches in what is now Union Square. He died at the age of 40. His sarcophagus may be found in the churchyard of the First Unitarian Church which is adjacent to this street.

STARVIEW Way: One of a number of streets in the residential subdivision, Midtown Terrace, which have "view" for their suffix.

STEINER Street: L. Steiner was a good friend of Charles Gough, who was a member of a committee that laid out and named streets in the Western Addition in 1855. Steiner's occupation in 1850 is not found today. He delivered water because there was no water system in San Francisco at that time.

STEUART Street: William M. Steuart came to California aboard the United States battleship Ohio in 1849. He was a member of the town council in 1849–50 and a delegate to, and acting chairman of, the California State Constitutional Convention at Monterey in 1849. The constitution guaranteed not only the right to pursue happiness but also the right to obtain it. Later, Steuart lost in an attempt to become governor.

STEVENSON Street: An officer of the First New York Volunteers, Colonel Jonathan Drake Stevenson arrived in California in March 1847 to fight in the Mexican War. Resigning from the army a year later, Stevenson turned to mining gold. He later bought real estate in Santa Cruz and San Francisco.

STILWELL Road: Probably named after "Vinegar Joe" or "Uncle Joe" Stilwell, the World War II general who was in charge of all US forces in the China, Burma, and Indian theatre of operations. At the start of hostilities in 1942, he headed both the United States and Chinese nationalist resistance, which tried to stop the Japanese advance on the Chinese mainland. After the war, Stilwell served as Sixth Army Commander until his death at the Presidio, where this street is located.

STOCKTON Street: Commodore Robert F. Stockton arrived in Monterey in command of the USS *Congress* eight days after Sloat took possession of California for the United States. He was appointed military governor of California, holding the post during the first six months of American jurisdiction. Stockton's grandfather was a member of the Continental Congress.

STONECREST Drive: A handsome name for a street in the Lakeside subdivision. The origin of the street name was inspired by the last name of the developers, Henry and Bill Stoneson.

STONEMAN Street: Possibly named after George Stoneman (1822–94) who was born in New York. He came to California in 1846 as a lieutenant in the Mormon battalion. He served with the Central Pacific Railroad survey in 1853, and with the Union Army as a general during the Civil War. He participated in the engagement at Chancellorsville and freed the Union prisoners at Andersonville. After the war, Stoneman returned to California where he was governor from 1883 to 1887.

STONEYBROOK Avenue: For the origin of this name see Stonecrest above. These brothers were also the developers of the Stoneson shopping complex which is a few blocks away.

STONEYFORD Avenue: See the above street name explanation.

STORRIE Street: In 1918, contractor Robert Storrie built this block-long street with debris left over from the construction of the Twin Peaks tunnel.

STRATFORD Drive: Probably named after Shakespeare's birthplace in England.

SUMMIT Street: This street sits atop one of the many hills in San Francisco. The number of hills depends upon what one considers to be a hill; however, most experts agree that the number varies between 10 and 42.

SUNRISE Way: The sunrise is visible from this street, if one is awake early enough, and there's no fog.

SUNSET Boulevard: Not named after Sunset Boulevard in Hollywood and Los Angeles, but after the San Francisco district through which this wide, tree-lined street passes. This neighborhood is in the extreme western part of San Francisco, where the sun sets into the Pacific Ocean.

SUNVIEW Drive: A view of the sun and the City below may be obtained from this street near Twin Peaks.

SURREY Street: Probably named after the county in southeastern England that adjoins the River Thames. Its name meant "southern district" in the Saxon language.

SUSSEX Street: Named after one of the kingdoms of Anglo-Saxon England, which is now known as the county of Sussex. This name is derived from the Old English *Suo Seax* or "South Saxons."

SUTRO HEIGHTS Avenue: Adolph Sutro, twenty-first mayor of San Francisco (1895–97), started out as a cigar dealer. Self-educated, Sutro became a noted mining engineer, winning fame and fortune by driving a five-mile tunnel into the Comstock Lode in Nevada. Several other landmarks are named for him, not the least of which is Mount Sutro. A great Jewish civic benefactor, Sutro sponsored tree plantings throughout the City.

SUTTER Street: In 1839, Swiss adventurer, John A. Sutter, arrived in Yerba Buena. The Mexican government granted him large holdings of land in the Sacramento Valley where he raised crops. In January 1848, a carpenter named James Wilson Marshall found a few flakes of gold while building a sawmill for Sutter, on the south fork of the American River at Colma. Marshall brought the gold to Sutter at the place now known as Sutter's Fort. The news soon leaked out, and the Gold Rush began. Curiously, both Sutter and Marshall ended their lives in poverty.

SWEENY Street: Surveyor John Sweeny was employed by the Crocker Building and Land Company in the 1880s during the subdividing of the Crocker estate. The estate was located where this street is, in the Outer Mission district.

SWISS Avenue: Probably named after a Swiss the pioneer. The two words, Swiss and Switzerland, are derived from Schwyz, one of the original cantons, or districts, of the country, which, along with two other districts, joined to form the nucleus of this nation in the 13th Century.

SYLVAN Drive: *Sylvan* is the Latin word for "forest." This street has several associations with trees. It ends at Eucalyptus and is located two blocks west of Forest View. But, aside from one palm tree, there are no other trees on this street.

T

TACOMA Street: This word is the Indian name for Mt. Rainier, Washington State's highest mountain.

TAMALPAIS Terrace: "Tamalpais" combines the Spanish word, *pais*, meaning "country" with the Miwok Indian word, *tamal* probably meaning "bay mountain." Since the Southern Coast Miwok Indians were also called "Tamales" by the Spaniards, it seems likely that originally this was the name of a village of the Tamal Indians at the foot of the mountain in Marin County and meant "the Tamales in the bay mountain country." (See also Mount Tamalpais in the Bay Area Landmarks section).

TANDANG SORA Street: Tandang Sora was a hero in the Philippine struggle against the Spanish in the 1890s. In 1979, the street name was changed from Lefty O'Doul Lane, which commemorated the San Francisco baseball player, who was first a pitcher, then an outfielder, and finally, a manager for the San Francisco Seals for 17 seasons.

TAPIA Drive: Felipe Santiago Tapia was a soldier and settler in San Jose from 1776 to 1790. Born in 1745 in Culiacan, he was chosen as a recruit for Captain Juan Anza's party of 1776. He brought his wife and nine children with him. They had five more children between 1778 and 1786.

TARA Street: Between the 1st and 4th centuries, Tara was the seat of the ruling clan of County Mead, Ireland.

TARAVAL Street: Taraval was Captain Juan Anza's Indian guide during the journey to northern California in 1776.

TAYLOR Street: (also Road) General Zachary Taylor (1784–1850) was the hero of the Battle of Buena Vista and twelfth President of the United States.

TEHAMA Street: There are two possibilities as to the origin of this name. One possibility is the word of Indian origin that means "high water." The Tehama Indian Tribe resided in what is now the northern part of the Sacramento Valley. The more likely explanation has to do with the street's early inhabitants. This street was made quite famous in the 1890s because many chorus girls who worked in the Old Tivoli House on Eddy Street lived along it. To compete with the wealthy women from Nob Hill, who were bedecked with diamonds and sealskin coats, these girls wore an imitation sealskin which was made from dog skins and cat fur. It was called "Tehama Sealskin." Although no one now knows why "tehama" as used to represent a fake skin, one can only speculate why this meaning was derived from the Spanish word, *tejamaní*, or "shingle."

TELEGRAPH HILL Boulevard: (also Telegraph Place) These streets received their names because they go to Telegraph Hill. (See Telegraph Hill in the Bay Area Landmarks section of this book.)

TEMESCAL Terrace: This Indian word of Aztec origin means "seat house." A *temescal* was an Indian sauna, a low dugout covered with rocks.

TEMPLE Street: This street bisects Saturn Street. Saturn's temple still stands (in part) in Rome, and this street may have been given this name to commemorate Saturn's temple.

TENNESSEE Street: The state and the river's name came from an important Cherokee town located on the Little Tennessee River and spelled variously *Tanase, Tennassee, Tanasi,* and *Tinasse.* The meaning of the name is unknown.

TERRA VISTA Avenue: The name combines the Latin *terra*, meaning "land" with the Spanish *vista*, meaning "view."

TERRY A. FRANCOIS Boulevard: An attorney, Terry Francois was the City's first African-American supervisor. His term of office ran from 1964 to 1978, and during that period he also acted at times as the City's first African-American mayor. Prior to his political career he headed the City's chapter of the NAACP. The street named in his honor was formerly part of China Basin Street.

TEXAS Street: The state's name comes from an Indian variation, *texia*, of the Spanish word *tejas*, meaning "allies," which was used by various tribes in reference to their mutually protective alliances.

THOMAS Avenue: General George H. Thomas was the commanding general of the Division of the Pacific from 1869 to 1870. Thomas participated in the Civil War. He died in San Francisco.

THOMAS MELLON Drive: A distinguished civil servant, Thomas Mellon was the City's chief administrative officer from 1964 through 1976. Prior to this appointment, he was president of the Chamber of Commerce. After his career in public service concluded, he became involved in the real-estate development of the Executive Office Park, which is where this street is located.

THOMAS MORE Way: Named for the Roman Catholic church, St. Thomas More, which was situated on this thoroughfare. Thomas More (1477–1535), the British humanist and statesman, was killed for refusing to accept King Henry VIII as head of the Church of England.

THOR Avenue: This deity was common to all early Germanic peoples and was also a great warrior. Thor was represented as a red-bearded, middle-aged man of enormous strength and an implacable foe of giants, but benevolent toward humankind.

TIFFANY Avenue: Robert J. Tiffany's story of overcoming adversity through perseverance was typical of many pioneers. In 1849 when news of the gold discoveries reached him, he left his native state of New York for California, and he arrived in San Francisco in 1850. An unlucky gold miner, he returned to New York. Returning to San Francisco in 1853, his luck changed when he opened a hat store that flourished. Tiffany bought land and became head of the People's Homestead, a property development firm, as well as a bank director, and president of the Association of California Pioneers in 1860.

TILLMAN Place: The Tillman family, which built safes, lived on this little alley.

TIOGA Alley: In the Iroquois language, *tioga* means "where it forks." The name was given to an Iroquois village in central Pennsylvania located where the Susquehanna river joins the Chemung River. It is also the name of a county in New York, which is probably the direct origin of this street name.

TOCOLOMA Avenue: In the central Sierra Miwok Indian language tokoloma means "land salamander." The street was named for a now-vanished town which flourished in west Marin County in the beginning of the 20th Century.

TOLAND Street: (also Place) Doctor Hugh Huga Toland was a noted surgeon (1806–1880), who pioneered corrective surgery for club feet. In 1853 Toland reached San Francisco, and he became known as "the great surgeon of the Pacific Coast." He founded Toland Medical College in San Francisco, which was turned over to the University of California in 1873.

TOLEDO Way: In 193 B. C., this city in south central Spain was captured by the Romans. As Toletum, it became an important Roman colony. The present name evolved from the Latin.

TOPEKA Avenue: The capital city of Kansas' name is of uncertain Indian origin. One interpretation is "smoky hill," while another is "a good place to dig potatoes." The Indian term may refer to any edible root, not specifically to potatoes.

TOVAR Avenue: Pedro Tovar was an officer in Coronado's army, which explored the Southwest.

TOWNSEND Street: In 1844, Doctor James Townsend came overland to California. Townsend was mayor of San Francisco for five months in 1848, and he was one of the City's leading citizens between 1845 and 1850.

TOYON Lane: This is the name of a beautiful shrub also known as Christmas berry and California holly. It is similar to the Spanish name for the evergreen plant *tollon*.

TRADER VIC Alley: The name was changed in 1985 to honor Vic Bergeron (1902–1984). He opened the first Trader Vic restaurant in 1934, across the Bay in Emeryville. After World War II, Bergeron created a series of such establishments featuring food from the Pacific Islands. One of the first such eateries was in this alley in San Francisco. As of this writing (1995), the restaurant is closed.

TRANSVERSE Drive: This road cuts across and runs through Golden Gate Park. A similarly named drive crosses Central Park in New York City.

TREAT Avenue: George Treat was an early settler who owned famous race horses. In his later years, Treat became interested in Mexican mining ventures.

TRENTON Street: Probably named after the capital city of New Jersey. In 1714, William Trent, a Philadelphia merchant, bought 800 acres and laid out the town which was named in his honor in 1721.

TRINITY Street: Named after the Holy Trinity.

TULANE Street: Named after the university in New Orleans. In the late 1860s many of the streets in the Excelsior District were named after colleges and universities by the land developers of the area, the University Homestead Association.

TUNNEL Avenue: This road runs adjacent to the Southern Pacific's tracks. At the street's end, these tracks enter a tunnel which burrows under one of San Francisco's nameless southern hills.

TURK Street: (also Boulevard) Lawyer Frank Turk came to San Francisco in 1849 and worked in the post office for John W. Geary. At the first election of local officers in that same year, Turk was elected to the office of second *alcalde* (magistrate). He later became a clerk of the town council. At one time, Turk owned nearly all of what is now known as Nob Hill.

TUSCANY Alley: Tuscany is the district in west central Italy whose name is derived from an Etruscan tribe who settled there around 1000 B.C. *Tuscia* came into official use as a name for this area under the Roman empire.

TWIN PEAKS Boulevard: See Twin Peaks in the Bay Area Landmarks section of this book.

UGARTE Street: During the latter part of the 17th Century, John Ugarte founded missions in Lower California.

ULLOA Street: Francisco de Ulloa was a navigator and a member of the Portolá expedition to northern California. The street was named by the developers of this part of the Sunset District, the Parkside Realty Company, around the turn of the 20th Century.

UNDERWOOD Avenue: Named for General Franklin Underwood, about whom little is known.

UNION Street: The origin of this street name is unknown. It appears on William Eddy's survey of 1849 and may refer to the Union of States which California joined, a year later when it became a state. If this is correct, it would appear to be a case of withful thinking. Union Square, however, did not receive its name until several years later.

UNIVERSITY Street: Named for and by the University Homestead Association, which developed this part of the Excelsior District in the late 1860s. This name originated from the fact that an academy, the University Mound College, was situated nearby. This institution started as a boys' high school in 1859.

UPPER Terrace: One of two such streets—the other is Lower Terrace—on the slopes of Mount Olympus whose names give a verbal sense of their spatial relationship.

UPTON Street: (also Avenue in the Presidio) Probably named for Matthias Gilbert Upton, who was a political and commercial force in early California and the principal editor and writer for one of San Francisco's first newspapers, *Alta California*.

URANUS Terrace: The personification of heaven in Greek mythology is the namesake of the planet Uranus. This street runs into another such street, Saturn, on the slopes of Mt. Olympus.

URBANO Drive: *Urbano* is Italian for "urbanized," but why it was selected at the name of this street is lost to history. This street is in the form of an oval and was once a race track for horses.

UTAH Street: The state's name is derived from the Indian name *Ute* or *Eutaw*, an Indian tribe that inhabited that area for more than a century. The word has been variously defined to mean "in the tops of the mountains," "high up," "the land of the sun," and "the land of plenty."

VALENCIA Street: Named either for José Manuel Valencia, a soldier in Captain Juan Anza's company, or for his son, Candelario Valencia, who served in the military at the Presidio and later owned a ranch in Lafayette in Contra Costa County. Candelario also owned property adjoining the Mission Dolores, located two blocks from this street.

VALLEJO Street: General Mariano Guadalupe Vallejo was commander of the Presidio in San Francisco in 1835. Later, General Vallejo remained active in the state's affairs and served as a member of California's Constitutional Convention of 1849. It was at Vallejo's Sonoma estate that California's short-lived "Bear Flag Republic" was proclaimed.

VALLEY Street: Although not quite in a valley, this street goes through the neighborhood known as Noe Valley.

VALPARAISO Street: In Portuguese this means "valley of paradise." There is also a city with this name in Chile which was named after a city in Spain. San Francisco's second surveyor, Jasper O'Farrell, who lived in the Chilean seaport in the 1840s before moving to San Francisco, selected this name.

VAN BUREN Street: Probably named after Martin Van Buren, eighth President of the United States (1837–41) and one of the founders of the Democratic party. Van Buren, known as the "Little Magician," was a skillful and cunning politician.

VAN DYKE Avenue: Lawyer Walter Van Dyke, a native of New York, came overland to California soon after the discovery of gold. The first elected district attorney of Trinity County, he was appointed US Attorney in 1873. Later, he became a justice of the Supreme Court of California.

VAN NESS Avenue: The widest street (125 feet) in San Francisco was named for James Van Ness, the mayor of San Francisco in 1856. In 1855, as an alderman he authored the ordinance that granted Western Addition land titles to the people who actually possessed the property. He ended his political career as a state senator in 1871.

VARELA Avenue: Casimiro Varela holds the distinction of being one of the first settlers of both San Francisco (1777) and Los Angeles (1790). Varela and his wife came with Captain Juan Anza's expedition to northern California in 1776. Their daughter, Marta, was born in 1778 in San Francisco.

VEGA Street: A common Spanish surname.

VENTURA Avenue: A shortened version of San Buenaventura, the leader of the Franciscan Order after St. Francis.

VENUS Street: In Roman mythology, the goddess of agriculture; her name became associated with beauty, charm, and the power of love.

VERMONT Street: The state's name comes from the French mont vert, or "green mountains." This is the second-most-crooked street in San Francisco, with five full, and two half, turns in the block between McKinley and 22nd streets on Potrero Hill.

VERONA Place: Probably named after the province and city in northern Italy. Founded by an ancient tribe, it became a Roman colony in 89 B.C. and rapidly rose in importance because of its strategic location between Rome and southern Europe.

VESTA Street: She is the beautiful Roman goddess of the hearth. Her name is derived from a Sanskrit root *ves*, which expresses the idea of "shining." Vesta also personified fire when it was used for domestic or religious ceremonies.

VIA BUFANO: (formerly Grover Place) Benjamino Bufano, the famous Italian-American sculptor, once had his studio near this alley. Perhaps his best-known monumental sculptures are located at San Francisco's International Airport, in front of Candlestick Park, at Longshoremen's Hall near Fisherman's Wharf, and at Fort Mason.

VIA FERLINGHETTI: (formerly Price Row) Lawrence Ferlinghetti is the owner of City Lights bookstore and has been a friend to poets, artists, and writers for many decades. He has published most of "The Beat" authors and was the motivating force in having a dozen of San Francisco street names changed to honor some of the City's creative residents.

VICENTE Street: Probably named for a member of Captain Juan Anza's expedition to San Francisco in 1776. Many streets in the outer Sunset district were named for early Spanish settlers by the developers, the Parkside Realty Company, around the turn of the 20th Century.

VICKSBURG Street: The Civil War Battle of Vicksburg took place near this city in Mississippi. The city was named to honor the Reverend Newitt Vick, a Methodist minister.

VICTORIA Street: Probably named either after the British Queen (1819–1901) whose long reign restored dignity and popularity to the British crown, and possibly saved the monarchy from abolition, or named for the ancient Roman goddess of victory, responsible for success in arms. Or possibly named for Manuel Victoria, one of the governors of northern California in the Mexican period.

VIDAL Drive: Mariano Vidal was a purveyor for and a member of Captain Juan Anza's expedition to northern California in 1776.

VIENNA Street: The Austrian capital's name first appeared as Weina in the *Salzburg Annals* in 881 A.D.

VILLA Terrace: Originally a Roman term for a country estate complete with house, grounds and subsidiary buildings, villa now also refers to a sumptuous suburban estate. Approximately two dozen houses share a superb view of the City from this street, which is terraced into Twin Peaks.

VIRGIL Street: The great Roman poet Virgil (70–19 B.C.), is best known for his epic, the Aeneid. This street is one block away from Horace Street, which is named for another Latin lyric poet.

VIRGINIA Avenue: Named after either the girl's name or the state, which was named for Elizabeth I, the "virgin queen."

VISITACION Avenue: The name came from the "visitation" of the Virgin Mary to Saint Elizabeth, the mother of John the Baptist. In 1839, Jacob P. Leese was granted a tract of land called Visitacion Valley, on which he was allowed to build houses. The street runs through this area and the street name is derived from this property, located in the southern part of San Francisco.

VISTA Court: This word means "view" in Spanish, but there is not much of one from this residential street in the Presidio.

VISTA VERDE Court: In Spanish this means "green view;" however, this name was probably selected for its sound rather than its meaning by the homeowners on this street who petitioned to change the name of this cul-de-sac at the end of Detroit Street.

WABASH Terrace: Probably named for the town and river in Indiana. The name is derived from an Indian word meaning "shining white" or "water over white stones."

WALLACE Avenue: William T. Wallace was appointed Chief Justice of the California Supreme Court in 1869. A Kentuckian who came west in 1852, Wallace first practiced law in San Jose and then became district attorney of Santa Clara County.

WALLEN Street: Brigadier General Henry D. Wallen fought in the Civil War and was the commanding officer of the Presidio in late 1865 and early 1866.

WALLER Street: R. H. Waller, the City recorder in the 1850s, was an early manager of the San Francisco Protestant Orphan Asylum. This institution was located on nearby Haight Street, from 1853 until shortly after the earthquake of 1906, when the building was razed.

WALTER U. LUM Place: (formerly Brenham Place) Walter Uriah Lum founded the *Chinese Times*, a popular newspaper. In 1904 Lum created the Chinese American Citizens Alliance, which fought for the repeal of the Chinese Exclusion Act, a discriminatory immigration law. Lum died in 1961, and 24 years later this street, which had been called Brenham Place, was renamed for him. He became the first Chinese person to be so honored.

WALTHAM Street: Possibly named after the city in Massachusetts, which was named for a town of the same name near London, England.

WASHINGTON Street: (also Boulevard) The first President of the United States, George Washington. The street names of Washington, Montgomery, Kearney, and Clay have been in continuous usage as street names longer than any others.

WATERLOO Street: The village in Belgium was the site of the battle between armies under Napoleon and the Duke of Wellington. Napoleon Street is nearby.

WAVERLY Place: The name is probably taken from the title of Sir Walter Scott's novel. There is also a street in New York with the same name. Originally, San Francisco's street was called Pike Street and was the location of "houses of ill repute." In the 1860s, the name was changed, but the street remained just as notorious.

WAWONA Street: According to some authorities, this is an Indian name which means "big tree." Around the turn of the 20th Century, it was selected to be the name of this street by the Parkside Realty Company, the developers of this outer Sunset district.

WAVERLY Place

WEBSTER Street: Named either for Daniel Webster (1782–1852), an orator, politician, and lawyer, who argued cases before the United States Supreme Court and served as a congressman, senator, and Secretary of State, or named for Noah Webster (1758–1843), a lexicographer, who is best known for his *American Spelling Book* (1783) and his *American Dictionary of the English Language* (1828).

WELSH Street: Captain Charles Welsh was born in 1810 and arrived in San Francisco in 1847. He built the first brick house in North Beach. He died in 1883.

WEST GATE Drive: You won't find a gate at this western entrance to Mount Davidson Manor, but in the 1920s, when this subdivision was built, this name suggested exclusivity and security.

WEST POINT Road: This street probably got its name because it is situated just west of Middle Point Road on the approach to Hunters Point.

WEST PORTAL Avenue: Portal is derived from the Latin word for "gate." This street is the western approach to the tunnel under Twin Peaks for the Muni Metro subway system, which runs all the way under Market Street.

WEST VIEW Avenue: There may have once been a view from this street, but there's not one now.

WESTBROOK Court: Elouise Westbrook was a prominent community leader in the 1960s at Hunters Point when the Redevelopment Agency's project there was developed.

WESTERN SHORE Lane: An appropriate name for a street in a housing project sponsored by the International Longshoremen's Union. The *Western Shore* was a three-masted, full-rigged ship built in 1874. Four years later, while bound for San Francisco from Puget Sound with a cargo of coal, this vessel was lost on Duxbury Reef. During her career, she held the record for the three fastest consecutive runs from Portland, Oregon to Liverpool, England, the fastest being in only 97 days.

WESTWOOD Drive: This residential subdivision has streets named after the points of the compass with the suffix "wood." This is the most westerly of these streets.

WHALESHIP Plaza: A type of vessel that was often found in Yerba Buena Cove. This harbor has now been filled in and is the present site of the Golden Gateway complex, where this plaza is located. Yankee whaleships plying the Pacific became common in the 1820s when the Japan whale grounds were discovered. These were fertile areas for hunting sperm whales. By the mid-1820s, the whaleships started to put in at San Francisco's harbor for beef, vegetables, wood, water, and other provisions.

WHIPPLE Avenue: Major General Emile W. Whipple died of battle wounds at Chancellorsville on May 4, 1863.

WHITFIELD Court: Geneva Whitfield was a prominent community leader in Hunters Point during the 1960s when the Redevelopment Agency's project was under construction.

WHITNEY YOUNG Circle: Whitney Young, an African-American civil rights leader, spearheaded the drive for equal opportunity for African-Americans in the United States during his ten years (1961–71) as head of the National Urban League.

WILDER Street: A popular and prominent citizen, James Wilder was one of the founders of the San Francisco tugboat business at the turn of the 20th Century. In 1869 he was saved at sea by George Dewey (see Dewey Avenue).

WILDWOOD Way: One of a series of streets in Westwood Highlands which have the suffix "wood."

WILLIAM SAROYAN Place: (formerly the eastern half of Adler Alley) *The Time of Your Life*, William Saroyan's most famous play, is set at a neighborhood saloon in nearby North Beach. Although Saroyan was born in Fresno, he spent much of his adulthood in San Francisco. In the late 1920s he lived at 2378 Sutter Street, 1707A Divisadero Street, and 348 Carl Street.

WILLIAMS Avenue: The college in Williamstown, Massachusetts is the namesake of this street in the Excelsior District, one of a number of streets in this area named after colleges and universities. The names were selected by the land developers, the University Homestead Association, in the late 1860s.

WINDSOR Place: This is an alley on Telegraph Hill adjacent to Castle Alley. Windsor Castle is one of the principal residences of the British royal family.

WINFIELD Street: This is one of the last brick streets in San Francisco. There are two possible versions for the origin of this street name. For the most probable interpretation see the entry for Scott Street. The other theory has it that the street was named for the Winfield family that once lived there. Before 1906, this street was called Chapultepec Street.

WISCONSIN Street: The state's name, which had been given to both the river and the frontier territory in 1836, is an anglicized version of a French rendering of an Indian word. According to one version, it means "our homeland," but other possibilities are "the gathering of the waters," and "a grassy place."

WOODHAVEN Court: This road is located in Forest Knolls, where the street names were conceived to evoke sylvan imagery.

WOODLAND Avenue: This street ends next to Sutro Forest. Presumably, there were more trees around it when it was named than there are now.

WOODSIDE Avenue: There are presently some woods located on one side of this street that runs by the Laguna Honda Home.

WOODWARD Street: Robert B. Woodward was a hotel keeper and the namesake of an unusual development. From 1866 to 1883, Woodward

Gardens stood near the location of this street at 13th and Mission streets. Woodward Gardens was a private pleasure resort with a public botanical garden, a playground, a skating area, a bandstand, a concert stage, an aquarium, an art gallery, a zoo, and a lake with boats for hire.

WORCESTER Avenue: Probably named for the city in Massachusetts, which was named after the city in England that is located in an area known as Worcestershire. This name may have come from William Worcester, an English topographer who lived in the 15th Century.

WRIGHT Loop: (also Street) Brigadier General George Wright was commander of the Department of the Pacific from 1862 to 1864, and commander of the District of California from 1864 to 1865. Wright drowned when the *Brother Jonathan* sank off the north coast of California on July 30, 1865.

YALE Street: The university was named for Eli Yale, who founded it in 1701. In the late 1860s many of the streets in the Excelsior District were named after eastern colleges and universities by the land developers, the University Homestead Association.

YERBA BUENA Avenue: In Spanish, this means "good herb." It was the original name for San Francisco from the time of its establishment as a village in 1834 until 1847. The Spanish thought this herb had beneficial medicinal qualities.

YORBA Street: Antonio Yorba was a sergeant of the Catalan volunteers with the Gaspar Portolá Expedition in 1769.

YORK Street: Probably named after New York City and State, which were named for the city in England located in the scenic vale of York. The adjacent street, Hampshire, was also named for a state that was named after an English district.

YORKE Way: Father Peter C. Yorke was the moving force behind one of San Francisco's bitterest and most bloody labor conflicts: the teamster-waterfront strike of 1901. The 37 year-old Father Yorke led the battle against the powerful employers' organization, the police, and other city authorities to protect the strike breakers. He turned public opinion to favor workers. In 1903, Yorke moved to Oakland, but returned to San Francisco in 1911 as pastor of St. Peter's Parish, a position he held until his death in 1925.

YOSEMITE Avenue: The name for the valley, the falls, and the national park was derived from the Native American word *oosoomate*, meaning "grizzly bear." The Yosemite Indians were called "grizzlies" by their enemies.

YUKON Street: The Alaskan river's and the territory in northwest Canada's name means "the river" or "big river" in the native Indian language.

ZAMPA Lane: This is an appropriate name for a street in a housing project sponsored by the International Longshoremen's Union. The *Zampa* was a three-masted schooner built in 1887 at Port Madison, Washington.

ZOE Road: This is the Greek word for "life." It is also a woman's name, so this street may have been named for a relative or friend of a pioneer.

BAY AREA LANDMARKS

ALCATRAZ ISLAND In 1775, Captain Juan Manuel de Ayala gave the name *Isla de Alcatraces*, or in English, "Pelican Island," to the island we now call Yerba Buena (or "good herb" in English). This piece of land is located in the bay next to Treasure Island between San Francisco and Oakland. A subsequent map maker misapplied the name of Alcatraz to a smaller, nearby, barren island in 1826. Alcatraz Island was an Army prison from 1859 to 1934; it held Indians, Confederates, and deserters. It became a federal prison in 1934. Among the more notorious inmates were Al Capone, who resided there from 1934 to 1939; Robert Stroud, better known as the "Birdman of Alcatraz" (1942–1959), who was the only public enemy personally arrested by J. Edgar Hoover; and Alvin Karpis, who had the dubious distinction of being the longest resident, with a 27-year stint, 1936–1963. The island is now part of the Golden Gate National Recreation Area and one of the most popular attractions in the entire National Park system.

ANGEL ISLAND Captain Juan Manuel de Ayala anchored off an island in 1775 that he called *La Isla de Nuestra Señora de los Angeles*, or "The Island of Our Lady of the Angels." The name was anglicized on maps as Angel Island in 1826, although it was also known as Wood Island and later as Los Angeles Island. About a mile square, this island has had a busy history. In the 1850s, President Fillmore declared the island a military reservation. Soldiers occupied the island from 1863 until 1962. From 1910 until 1940, Angel Island was also used as an immigration processing center, and it became known as the "Ellis Island of the West." Thousands of Asian immigrants were processed here from 1910 until 1940. A quarantine station concurrently existed on this island from 1892 until 1939. It is now a state park.

BAKERS BEACH The Baker family's dairy ranch was known as the Golden Gate Ranch in the 1860s. Located on the edge of what was the ranch, this beach is tucked between what is now Lincoln Park and the Golden Gate

Bridge. Typical of all of San Francisco's beaches, the ocean water is too cold to swim in, but the sunbathing is just fine on a warm spring or fall day.

CANDLESTICK PARK Adjacent to Candlestick Cove, this stadium is on land which was named for a tall offshore rock that looked like a candelabra. This land form later disappeared. The name of the area remained even though most of the cove was filled in by the State Highway Department in 1954 to build a freeway. It was opened on April 12, 1960 and is now the second oldest baseball park in the National League. It is famed for its brisk winds, bad weather, and struggling baseball team. In 1995, the name of the stadium was changed to 3Com Park, but only time will tell if this name prevails.

THE CANNERY This complex of shops and restaurants was originally the canning factory for the Del Monte Fruit Company. The only remnant of this ownership is the Del Monte logo, a star in a circle, which may be seen atop the building.

CHINATOWN Chinese settlers have lived in this part of the City since its beginning. Driven from Kwangtung province in southern China by civil war and famine, the Chinese arrived by the thousands in the 1850s. Many worked in the gold country, while others came to work on the Central Pacific Railroad. They were called "Crocker's Pets," because Charles Crocker, one of the owners of the railroad, masterminded their immigration. These immigrants were subjected to intense racial harassment during the depression of the "Terrible 70s." Most of them settled in Chinatown, where some opened restaurants and laundries. For years, these new Americans were a major manual labor pool in this City.

COIT TOWER (on Telegraph Hill) Lillie Hitchcock Coit left funds to beautify the City when she died at the age of 86 in 1929. She wanted the City to create a memorial to the volunteer firemen. As a young girl, Lillie was a mascot of a fire engine house, Knickerbocker Company Number 5. When she grew older, she became one of the City's grandest eccentrics, with a reputation for chasing after fire engines and visiting the Barbary Coast in male clothes. In 1933 her gift was used to build Coit Tower. Above the entrance to the tower is a relief plaque of the Phoenix, the mythical bird reborn in fire, which is also San Francisco's symbol, appearing on the city's flag and seal. Contrary to public opinion, the Phoenix does not symbolize San Francisco's rebirth after the fire of 1906, but instead it commemorates the many deadly fires and rebirths of the Gold Rush years.

CONTRA COSTA COUNTY In chauvinistic San Francisco this is an appropriate name for the land on the other side of the Bay: "the opposite coast."

COW HOLLOW Cows were once pastured in this area, which was watered by the little creeks from the surrounding hills. These fields boasted a respectable natural growth of grass, which improved the more it was pastured. Early San Francisco's milk came from Cow Hollow. During the 1860s, George Hatman began a dairy ranch on several acres in this area; by the 1880s, the Board of Health ordered all the cattle in the City to be moved to less populous areas.

DALY CITY John Daly subdivided his dairy farm after the earthquake and fire of 1906. It was located south of San Francisco, where Daly City is now.

FARALLON ISLANDS This word in Spanish means "cliff,"and these seven islands have them. Even though they are 32 miles out in the Pacific Ocean, they are a part of the City and County of San Francisco. They are inhabited only by birds, sea lions, and seals. They were originally called the "Islands of Saint James" by Drake (1579); the Sebastian Vizcaíno expedition (1602–03) renamed them "the Friars." In 1775, Juan Francisco de Bodega y Quadra, another Spanish explorer, called these islands *Farallones de los Frayles*, or "cliffs or small pointed islands in the sea of the friars." The present name is an Americanized contraction of Bodega's appellation. During the Gold Rush, wild bird eggs from the Farallon Islands were sold for one dollar each in San Francisco.

FISHERMAN'S WHARF This is the home of San Francisco's commercial fishing fleet, where the fishermen return with their daily catch, which often includes anchovies, striped bass, sole, sand dabs, and, of course, crabs. As a tourist attraction, this area is the second-most-popular destination in California, surpassed only by Disneyland.

FORT FUNSTON Named to honor Major General Frederick Funston (1865–1917), a hero of the Spanish-American War. He was in command of the Department of California at the time of the earthquake and fire in 1906. The fort, situated along the Pacific Coast in the southwestern part of the City, is a popular spot for hang-gliders.

FORT MASON In 1882, this military reservation was named for Colonel Richard B. Mason, the military governor of California after the American occupation and during the discovery of gold. His reports confirmed the existence of gold and set off the Gold Rush. Fort Mason is now, in part, a cultural center, housing scores of art galleries, museums, theaters, and offices for non-profit groups.

FORT MILEY Named to honor Lieutenant Colonel John D. Miley who died in Manila on September 19,1899, during the Spanish-American War.

FORT POINT When Captain Juan Manuel de Ayala sailed past this piece of land at the entrance to the Bay in 1775, he named it *Punta de San José*. Later, when this site became a Spanish fort guarding the approach to Yerba Buena, it was called *Castillo de San Joaquin*. In 1851, the Coast Survey discovered the ruins of this fort and they decided to call this area Fort Point, in part after Ayala's original name for the area. The present fort was built as a part of the Presidio between 1853 and 1861, on the site of the earlier structure. The run—or walk—from the Embarcadero to Fort Point is one of the most magnificent in the world.

GHIRARDELLI SQUARE In 1897, Domingo Ghirardelli moved his chocolate and spice factory to this location on North Point Street, taking over the brick buildings abandoned by the Columbia Woolen Mills. The factory complex was transformed into the present array of shops and restaurants by William Matson Roth in the late 1960s.

GOLDEN GATE Although the area is frequently covered by fog, pioneer explorer John Frémont was so impressed with its beauty in 1846 that he named it, in his words, "Chrysopylae or Golden Gate, for the same reason that the harbor of Byzantium was called Chrisoceras or Golden Horn." Today, it is the site of the tallest, and second-longest, span steel bridge in the world, which connects Marin County with San Francisco. The Golden Gate Bridge was the only major public project built in the United States without federal aid.

HUNTERS POINT This name comes from one of two possible sources. In 1849, Robert E. Hunter and his brother, Philip, participated in a project to develop a city on this point of land, which was to be called South San Francisco. Alternatively, this area may be known as Hunters Point because sportsmen went hunting there.

LAKE MERCED Named after The Feast of Our Lady of Mercy by the Franciscan Brother Palóu, when the Heceta expedition arrived on its shores on or about September 24, 1775.

MARIN COUNTY There are two versions concerning the origin of the name. One likely possibility is that it was named after a captured Indian who became such an outstanding navigator that he was called *El Marinero*, or "The Sailor." The other explanation is that the name was originally applied to Marin Island, a small island in San Francisco Bay, by an Indian who lived on it. This Indian may have gotten the name from Spanish explorers, who called the bay in which this island lies, *Bahia de la Marinera*. Consequently, the name, Marin, may actually have been derived from this earlier name for the bay. See also Marin Street.

MISSION DOLORES This mission is actually named Mission San Francisco de Asís and it was dedicated on October 9, 1776, by Brother Francisco Palóu. The mission is one of the 21 that were established by the Franciscans along the California coast from San Diego, where the first was erected by Father Junípero Serra on July 16, 1769, to Sonoma, which was constructed in 1823. The San Francisco Mission acquired its popular name from the *Laguna de Nuestra Señora de Los Dolores*, a nearby lake that was named after the "Virgin of Sorrows," because the Spanish explorers discovered it on her feast day, but the lake no longer exists. Although a few bricks remain of an earlier adobe structure at the Officers' Club in the Presidio, Mission Dolores is the oldest intact building in San Francisco.

MOUNT DAVIDSON George Davidson, a government surveyor, surveyed the peak in 1852 and called it Blue Mountain. It was renamed in 1911, and at 927 feet it is the highest point in the City. It is the site of the annual sunrise Easter services which are held on top of the mountain at the foot of a 103-foot concrete cross.

MOUNT DIABLO This is the Spanish word for "devil." The mountain was named by Spanish explorers after they encountered an Indian medicine man in a skirmish who looked like "the devil himself" in his battle attire.

MOUNT OLYMPUS One story indicates that this hill was named for "Old Limpus" Hanrahan, a crippled neighborhood milk peddler. Another version suggests that it was named after Mount Olympus in Greece, because it had a view that was "fit for the gods."

MOUNT TAMALPAIS The Tamales were Indians living in what is now Marin County, and it is believed that their name refers to "bay mountain." In Spanish, *pais* means "country." This name may mean "the people living at the base of the bay mountain country." (See also Tamalapais Terrace.)

MOUNTAIN LAKE This body of water was originally called *Laguna de Loma Alta*, the "Lake of the High Hill," referring to the 400-foot elevation of the site where this lake is located. Mountain Lake was first observed by members of Captain Juan Anza's party when they explored this area in 1776.

NAPA COUNTY An Indian word for either "house," "motherland," or "grizzly bear."

NOB HILL The area was first called "Fern Hill," then "Clay Street Hill" and later "California Street Hill." There are two possible explanations for the origin of the present name. One is that "Nob" is a contraction of the word "knob," meaning an isolated rounded hill or mountain; this would appear to be a logical name for this 338-foot hill. Another, and perhaps more likely, possibility is derived from the fact that wealthy San Franciscans—called "nabobs" and later maybe shortened to "nobs"—lived here in the 1870s and 1880s. "Nabob" is a British slang word for a "wealthy person." It comes from the Hindu *nawwah* meaning "governor" or "vice-agent." The word was used by the English to describe the ostentatious excolonists who returned to Great Britain with riches acquired in India. Nob Hill's first residence was built on Mason Street near Sacramento Street by Dr. Arthur Hayne in 1856. Several great mansions were found here, but all but one were destroyed by the great fire of 1906. The home that remained was the Flood mansion, which was built of Connecticut brownstone. It now houses the Pacific Union Club at Mason and California Streets. Diagonally across the street is the block which was the site of the Hopkins mansion (now the site of the Mark Hopkins Hotel) and the Stanford mansion (now the site of the Stanford Court Hotel). The Crocker mansion became the site of the Grace Episcopal Cathedral at Taylor and California streets, and diagonally opposite this site is the Huntington Hotel, once the location of the Huntington mansion. Across the street from this home sat the Colton mansion, now the site of Huntington Park.

NORTH BEACH The name originated in the 1850s when a finger of the bay extended far inland between Telegraph and Russian hills. The neighborhood along this sunny stretch of shore was called North Beach. It has been the historic home of San Francisco's Italian community.

PEACE PLAZA A landmark at the Japanese Cultural and Trade Center that was designed to symbolize the amicable relationship between the United States and Japan. It was dedicated on March 28, 1968.

PETALUMA In the Miwok Indian language this word means "flat back" or "flat place."

PORTSMOUTH PLAZA Until 1927 this area was called Portsmouth Square. On July 9, 1846, it was the center of activity for the more than thirty residents of Yerba Buena when Captain John Montgomery disembarked from his vessel, the war sloop *Portsmouth*, and raised the United States flag. Once on the waterfront, the land has been filled in and now this area is the site of a small park.

POTRERO HILL The top of this hill once served as a *potrero* for the cattle of Mission Dolores. In Spanish this word means "pasture."

PRESIDIO This is the Spanish word for "garrison" or "fortified barracks." The Presidio of San Francisco was established in 1776 and was a military post continuously until 1995. It was the largest and oldest urban military installation in the country and it is a national landmark. It was the headquarters of the now deactivated United States Sixth Army. When the army left, the land became part of the Golden Gate National Recreational Area.

RICHMOND This district in San Francisco was named after a house which once stood at 12th Avenue and Clement Street. The house was owned by George Marsh who moved to the area in 1875. Marsh was born in Richmond, Australia, and he named his home after his birthplace. Marsh's ancestors emigrated to Australia from Richmond, England, and the name of this community is derived from the castle called Richmond, which is located on the Thames River.

RINCON HILL Yerba Buena Cove was once located where we find the Ferry Building today, at the foot of Market Street. Early settlers referred to its southern tip as Rincon (Spanish for "corner") Point and the hill rising from its base as Rincon Hill. This hill is located under the approach ramp of the Bay Bridge. From the mid 1850s until the early 1880s, this area was one of the City's most fashionable neighborhoods. In 1869 its demise began when it ceased being isolated from "downtown." This occurred when Rincon Hill was cut through and Second Street, once the area's main shopping street, was extended. The appearance of laborers' tents nearby and the proximity to noxious industries created by this new street hastened the change from a quality residential district to a commercial one.

RUSSIAN HILL One undocumented story suggests that this area was named after the Russian soldiers and/or sailors who were buried near the top of this 312-foot hill in the City's early days. In the middle of the 19th Century children, playing amongst the graves, began to refer to the hill as "Russian."

SAN FRANCISCO Originally called *El Paraje de Yerba Buena*, "The Place of the Good Herb," the village's name was changed to San Francisco on January 30, 1847. The name was selected by Washington A. Bartlett, a Spanish-speaking lieutenant on the USS *Portsmouth*, who had become the most important municipal officer in town. The name was selected to honor the bay on which the town was situated and the nearby Mission

San Francisco de Asís, better known as Mission Dolores. Although Bartlett lacked the authority, he published his proclamation in *The California Star*, and on January 30, 1847, the American military governor made the new name official. There is no compelling reason for the city of San Francisco to have become the great nexus of California during the Gold Rush. that later became Oakland across the Bay would have done just as well, as might have Benicia at the Carquinez Strait. In fact, it was word of a move by some early settlers to develop a town called Francisca at what is now Benicia that inspired Bartlett to select the name. (See also San Francisco Bay, below.)

SAN FRANCISCO BAY The name "San Francisco" came about through a geographical mix-up. In 1575, the Spanish sailor Sebastian Cermeño landed at what is today known as Drake's Bay, part of Point Reyes and approximately 30 miles north of what is now San Francisco. He named this body of water in honor of the founder of the Franciscan order, St. Francis of Assisi. Because fog frequently obscures the entrance to San Francisco Bay from the Pacific Ocean, neither Cermeño nor the subsequent English explorer, Sir Frances Drake, observed the large harbor, a few miles to the south. When the Bay was finally discovered in 1769 by José Ortega, he mistook it for Cermeño's (or Drake's) bay and therefore gave it that bay's Spanish name. One of the world's greatest natural harbors, San Francisco Bay today encompasses slightly more than 400 square miles. Despite its size it is remarkably shallow. Two-thirds of the Bay is less than 18 feet deep at low tide. Much of the Bay has been reclaimed, a practice which stopped in the 1970s. The Bay was originally 600-square miles, but now much of San Francisco's downtown and Marina district, as well as its International Airport, along with Foster City on the peninsula, the Berkeley waterfront, and other Bay-front enclaves lie on filled land which was once part of the Bay.

SAN QUENTIN A renegade Indian, Quinten was captured in the area in 1824. Ten years later, a Spanish land grant, *Rancho Punta de Quintin*, was named for him. The name was changed to the present spelling in the 1850s, when the American mapmakers added "San," "Santa," and "Santo" to many names whether or not the person was a saint. Now it is the name for, and site of, an overcrowded state prison.

SAN RAFAEL This town, now the county seat of Marin, was named by the Franciscan monks for St. Rafael, the angel of body healing. The name was originally given to Mission San Rafael, which was an offshoot of San Francisco's Mission Dolores.

SAUSALITO Derived from the Spanish word *sauce*, which means "willow." This is a reference to the willow trees growing along the streams in this area. The term was used by Captain Juan Ayala in referring to this place in 1775. The correct Spanish name, *Saucelito*, appears in 1826 and was used for the land grant to William A. Richardson in 1838. Since then, the spelling of the name went through many changes until the present one was applied when the town was incorporated in 1893.

SONOMA COUNTY An Indian word for "nose," which may refer either to a nose-shaped landscape feature or to a local chief with a prominent proboscis. (See Sonoma Street.)

TIBURON The peninsula on which this town is located, and after which it takes its name, probably comes from the Spanish *ponte de tiburon,* or "shark's point," because of its physical resemblance to a shark nose on a map.

TELEGRAPH HILL From early in 1849, a signal announcing the arrival of ships was located on top of this hill. In September 1853, the first telegraph line in California, six miles in length, was completed. It connected Point Lobos at the Golden Gate with what became known as Telegraph Hill. It is one of the City's most visited hills because of the spectacular view of the Bay, visible from its 295-foot peak. Much of the rock on the east face of the hill was quarried between 1885 and 1901. The rock was used for many purposes, such as bulkhead ballast to stabilize empty homeward-bound boats, or for street paving.

TENDERLOIN DISTRICT Named after the comparable district in New York City that got its name from the tradition of paying higher wages to the police who worked in the riskier, more crime-infested areas. This bonus enabled these officers to afford more expensive cuts of meat.

TREASURE ISLAND When it was built in the late 1930s, this was the largest manmade island in the world, with 403 acres. The land was silt dredged from the shoals of the bay. Situated just north of Yerba Buena Island and originally constructed as an airport, in 1939 it became the site of the Golden Gate International Exposition. From World War II until the end of the cold war, the island was used as a naval base, until its deactivation in 1997. There are three versions concerning the origin of the name. One possibility is that many persons believed the silt drawn from the shoals contained flecks of gold that had been washed down stream from the Mother Lode. Another version maintains that the name was selected "because it expressed a glamorously beautiful, almost fabulous island that would present the treasures of the world." The third explanation suggests that it was named after the book written in 1883 by Robert Louis Stevenson.

TWIN PEAKS An Indian legend says that Twin Peaks was originally one mountain (man and wife) split into two by the Great Spirit with a bolt of lightning because the couple was so argumentative. When the Spanish came to Yerba Buena they referred to the peaks as *Los Pechos de la Choca,* in English "The Breasts of the Indian Maiden." One of San Francisco's most stunning views can be seen from atop Twin Peaks—the second and fourth tallest hills in San Francisco (910 and 904 feet).

UNION SQUARE This park was given to the city by Mayor John Geary in 1850. Eleven years later, a large public meeting was held in this park to decide whether or not San Francisco should secede during the Civil War. The placards in the square quoted Daniel Webster and said, "The Union, the whole Union and nothing but the Union" and "Liberty and Union,

Now and Forever, One and Inseparable." The square became the recognized rallying ground of Unionists, led by Edward Baker and the Unitarian minister Thomas Starr King.

WESTERN ADDITION In the 1860s, Larkin Street was the western boundary of the city. when a subsequent series of new projects went up west of the town's border, the newly developed area became know as the Western Addition.

YERBA BUENA ISLAND Yerba Buena was the original name for San Francisco. In Spanish it means "good herb". The name came from the wild mint which grew all over the sand dunes once found on this island, located south of Treasure Island in the middle of the Bay.

If you have information or a favorite story that corrects the information given, or explains the origin of a street name not listed here, please write to me in care of Wilderness Press, 1200 5th Street, Berkeley, CA 94710-1306 or email: mail@wildernesspress.com.

Louis K. Loewenstein

APPENDIX

Throughout their history, San Francisco streets have had frequent name changes. In the earliest years, Pacific Avenue was called Bartlett, Sacramento was named Howard, and Battery was called Sloat. Patriots in World War I renamed Berlin Street to be Brussels Street; during World War II, Japan Street became Colin P. Kelly Street.

Many of these changes are mentioned in the text, where I was able to discover the origins of the current (or the past) name. But almost two hundred streets exist whose name origins are lost to history. Often the only record available is the date of a name change—for instance, when Treat Alley was renamed Trainor in 1909.

Below, I have listed name changes which were not mentioned in the text. Unfortunately, the reasons for the changes were never recorded. Many were made to clear up confusion between streets, alleys, and places, but just as frequently, the motive seems to have been historical or even (as in the case of plain Mary Street transformed to illustrious Homer) whimsical.

Current Name	Previous Name	Date Changed
Abbey Street	Alemany Street	1909
Acton Street	Henrietta Street	1882
Addison Street	Lewis Street	1882
Adelle Court	Ade Alley	1928
Alert Court	Albert Alley	1909
Ames Street	Alder Alley	1909
Amity Alley	Ada Alley	1909
Anson Place	Ankeny Place	1909
Anthony Street	New Anthony Street	1909
Appleton Avenue	West Avenue	1909
	(was Hudson Street	1882)
Ashton Avenue	Arlington Avenue	1909
Banks Street	Ward Street	1882
Barneveld Street	Railroad Avenue	1882
Beaver Street	Tilden Street	1909
Beckett Street	Bartlet Alley	1909
Bennington Street	Scott Street	1882
Berwick Place	Mariposa Terrace	1909
Beverly Street	Thorton Street	1909
Bishop Street	Burnside Street	1909
Black Place	Bay View Place	1909
Bolana Street	North Avenue	1909
Boutwell Street	Hampshire Street	1882

Current Name	Previous Name	Date Changed
Boylston Street	King Street	1882
Boyton Court	Belcher Court	1909
Bradford Street	Mercer Street	1895
Brant Alley	Broad Alley	1909
Breen Place	Browns Alley	1909
Brice Terrace	Bryant Terrace	1909
Bromley Place	Webster Place	1909
Brompton Avenue	Fulton Avenue	1909
Bronte Street	Harrison	1882
Brush Place	Bruce Place	1909
Bruke Avenue	Second Avenue South	1909
Burnside Avenue	Kingston Avenue	1882
Butte Place	Brannan Place	1909
Byxbee Street	Ford Street	1882
Campbell Avenue	Barry Street	1909
Campton Place	Stockton Place	1909
Central Avenue	Lott Street	1895
Cherney Street	Glenn Avenue	1909
Child Street	Good Children Street	1909
Chilton Avenue	Clinton Avenue	1909
Churchill Street	Church Avenue	1909
Claude Lane	Clara Lane	1909
Clifford Terrace	Sixteenth Street	1909
Clyde Street	Liberty Street	1909
Coleridge Street	California Avenue	1909
Collingwood Street	Sherman Street	1882
Columbia Square Street	Columbia Street	1882
Conkling Street	Vermont Street	1882
Cordelia Street	Virginia Place	1882
Corwin Street	Stanton Street	1909
Cosmo Place	Lewis Place	1909
Cowell Place	Flint Alley	1909
Crystal Street	Milton Street	1882
Cumberland Street	Columbia Street	1882
Cunningham Place	Cumberland Place	1909
Cushman Street	Yerba Buena Street	1909
Cyrus Place	Morse Place	1909
Daggett Sreet	South Street	1909
Danvers Street	Rose Street	1882
Darrell Place	Norton Avenue	1909
Delano Avenue	Delaware Avenue	1909
Deming Street	Eighteenth Street	1909
Derby Street	Oak Street	1882
Drummond Street	Eureka Alley	1909
Eastman Street	West End Alley	1909
Edgardo Street	Edgar Stree	1909
Ellington Avenue	Porter Avenue	1909
Emerson Street	Obsidiana Lane	1970
Ewing Place	Metcalf Place	1882

Current Name	Previous Name	Date Changed
Fargo Place	Columbia Place	1882
Fielding Street	Newell Street	1882
Fitzgerald Avenue	Thirtieth Avenue South	1909
Flournoy Street	Prim Street	1924
Garfield Street	Sherman Street	1882
Gorham Street	Garden Lane	1912
Granville Way	Grafton Street	1913
Grote Place	Grant Place	1909
Grover Place	Gavin Place	1909
Hallam Street	Harrison Avenue	1909
Hamerton Avenue	Hamilton Avenue	1909
Harlow Street	Hardy Street	1909
Harper Street	Bartlett Street	1882
Hastings Terrace	Lincoln Place	1909
Havelock Street	Henry Street	1882
Head Street	Florence Street	1882
Highland Avenue	East Avenue	1909
Hilton Street	Lee Street	1909
Holladay Street	Heath Street	1909
Homer Street	Mary Street	1882
Ils Lane	Maiden Lane	1922
James Alley	Jackson Alley	1909
Jarobe Avenue	Jefferson Avenue	1909
Jasper Place	Union Place	1909
Jerrold Avenue	Tenth Avenue South	1909
Judson Avenue	Wieland Avenue	1899
Keith Street	K Street South	1909
Lamartine Street	Cotta Street	1909
Lansing Street	Laurel Place	1909
Lawrence Avenue	Sherman Avenue	1909
Ledyard Street	Emma Street	1882
Leona Terrace	Lyon Terrace	1909
Levant Street	Juno Street	1914
Linda Street	Angelica Street	1945
Lippard Avenue	Park Avenue	1882
Locksley Avenue	Serpentine Road	1909
Lowell Street	Humbolt Street	1882
Lucky Street	Garfield Avenue	1909
Lusk Street	Crooks Street	1961
Marcy Place	Vernon Place	1882
Margrave Place	Margaret Place	1909
Marston Avenue	Milton Avenue	1909
Maynard Street	Marshall Street	1909
Merlin Street	Madison Street	1909
Miguel Street	San Miguel Street	1938
Miller Place	Miles Place	1909
Montague Place	Moulton Place	1909
Murray Street	South Avenue	1909
Newburg Street	New Grove Avenue	1909

Current Name	Previous Name	Date Changed
Niantic Avenue	East Railroad Avenue	1912
Nordhoff Street	Midway Street	1909
Oakdale Avenue	Fifteenth Avenue South	1909
Ogden Avenue	Old Hickory Street	1909
Ordway Street	Irving Street	1882
Osgood Place	Ohio Avenue	1909
Otsego Avenue	West Lake Avenue	1909
Parkhurst Avenue	Parker Alley	1909
Parsons Street	Parkside Avenue	1909
Paulding Street	Paul Street	1909
Payson Street	Park Way	1909
Peabody Street	Byrne Street	1882
Pelton Place	Pacific Alley	1909
Powers Avenue	Powell Avenue	1909
Pratt Place	Ellick Lane	1913
Prescott Court	Ohio Avenue	1882
Quane Street	Quince Alley	1909
Ramsell Street	State Street	1882
Randall Street	Palmer Street	1909
Ridgewood Avenue	Hamburg Street	1927
Ripley Street	Prospect Place	1882
Rockdale Drive	San Martin Avenue	1939
Rockland Street	Brady Place	1882
Rodgers Street	Folsom Alley	1909
Romolo Place	Pinkey Place	1913
Roscoe Street	Decatur Street	1882
Rosemont Place	Maple Court	1909
Rowland Street	St. Charles Street	1882
Rutland Street	Allen Street	1882
Sabin Place	Salina Place	1909
Santa Rosa Avenue	Croke Street	1911
Sargent Street	Central Street	1882
Sawyer Street	Fay Street	1909
Severn Street	Medway Alley	1909
Shannon Street	William Street	1909
Sloan Alley	Tehama Alley	1909
Southard Place	Randall Place	1909
Spring Street	Webb Street	1909
Staples Avenue	Spreckels Avenue	1909
Stark Street	Polk Street	1882
Stillman Street	Silver Street	1909
Taber Place	Park Lane North	1909
Tenny Place	Tehama Place	1909
Thomas Avenue	Twentieth Avenue	1909
Thrift Street	Hill Street	1882
Tomkins Avenue	Union Avenue	1909
Tracy Place	Vallejo Alley	1909
Trainor Street	Treat Alley	1909
Treasury Place	Burnett Place	1909

Current Name	Previous Name	Date Changed
Trumbull Street	Lewis Street	1882
Valmar Terrace	Moscow Street	1955
Varennes Street	Lafayette Place	1909
Varney Place	Park Lane South	1909
Verdi Place	Montgomery Court	1909
Vinton Court	Virginia Court	1909
Wall Place	Coolidge Place	1912
Warner Place	Vernon Place	1909
Washburn Street	Washington Avenue	1909
Waterville Street	Nebraska Avenue	1882
Wayne Place	Scott Place	1909
Wentworth Street	Washington Place	1909
Wetmore Street	Tay Street	1923
Whitney Street	Palmer Street	1909
Wiese Street	Linda Place	1916
Willard Street	Belmont Avenue	1909
Willard Street North	Willard Street	1882
Wilmont Street	Widley Avenue	1909
Wilson Street	Bismarck Street	1924
Winthrop Street	Webster Street	1882
Woodland Avenue	Lotta Street	1909

In 1882, the following streets and alleys were given names. The reasons why these particular names were selected are lost.

Acorn Alley	Ophir Alley
Ada Court	Orange Alley
Alder Alley (now Street)	Oscar Alley
Clarion Alley	Pardee Alley
Eaton Alley (now Place)	Pink Alley
Edgar Place	Piper Loop
Fisher Alley	Redfield Alley
Golden Court	Shaw Alley
Harlem Alley	Spencer Alley (now Street)
Hobart Alley	Tehama Alley
Jerome Alley	Troy Alley
Malden Alley	Tulip Alley
Mersey Alley (now Street)	Wagner Alley
Opal Place	Waldo Alley

BIBLIOGRAPHY

Books

Alotta, Robert, *Street Names of Philadelphia*. Philadelphia: Temple University Press, 1975.

Bakalinsky, Ada, *Stairway Walks in San Francisco*. 3rd ed. Berkeley: Wilderness Press, 1995.

Block, Eugene B., *The Immortal San Francisco*. San Francisco: Chronicle Books, 1971.

Boatner, Martin M., *The Civil War Dictionary*. New York: David McKay Co., Inc. 1959.

Brown, Marion, *San Francisco Old and New*. San Francisco: The Grabhorn Press, 1939.

Carlisle, Henry C., *San Francisco Street Names*. San Francisco. American Trust Co., 1954.

Cassady, Stephen, *Spanning the Gate*. Mill Valley, CA: Square Books, 1979.

Cole, Tom, *A Short History of San Francisco*. San Francisco: Lexikos, 1981.

Conrad, Barnaby, *San Francisco: A Profile with Pictures*. New York: Viking Press, Inc., 1959.

Cowen, Robert G, *Ranchos of California*. Fresno, CA: Academy Library Guild, 1956.

Delehanty, Randolph, *San Francisco*. New York: The Dialogue Press, 1980.

Dolon, Bill and Karen Warner, *San Francisco Trivia*. San Francisco: 101 Productions, 1985.

Doss, Margaret Patterson, *San Francisco at Your Feet*. New York: Grove Press, 1964.

Eldredge, Zoeth S., *The Beginnings of San Francisco*, Volume II. New York: John Rankin, Co., 1912.

Encyclopedia Britannica. Chicago: Fifteenth Edition, 1974.

Ferlinghetti, Lawrence and others, *Names of 12 San Francisco Streets Changed to Honor Authors and Artists*. San Francisco, CA: City Lights Books, 1989.

Gudde, Erwin G., *California Place Names*. Berkeley, CA: University of California Press, 1949.

Hanna, Phil Townsend, *The Dictionary of California Land Names.* Los Angeles: The Automobile Club of Southern California, 1951.

Hansen, Gladys, *The San Francisco Almanac.* San Francisco: Chronicle Books, 1978, 1995.

_____, *The San Francisco Almanac.* Novato: Presidio Press, 1980.

Harder, Kelsie B., editor, *Illustrated Dictionary of Place Names: United States and Canada.* New York: Facts on File Publications, 1985.

Hart, James, *A Companion to California.* New York: Oxford University Press, 1978.

Kinnaird, Lawrence, *History of the Greater San Francisco Bay Region.* New York: Lewis Historical Publishing Company, 1966.

Larousse Encyclopedia of Mythology. New York: Prometheus Press, 1959.

Levinson, John, *Cow Hollow.* San Francisco: San Francisco Yesterday, 1976.

Lockwood, Charles, *Suddenly San Francisco.* San Francisco: California Living Book, 1978.

Lotchin, Rodger W., *San Francisco 1846–1856: From Hamlet to City.* New York: Oxford University Press, 1974.

McCarthy, Rev. Frances T., *Hunters Point.* San Francisco: Flores Paramount Press, 1942.

McDowell, Jack, editor, *San Francisco.* Menlo Park, CA: Lane Magazine and Book Company, 1969.

McGloin, John B., *San Francisco, The Story of a City.* San Rafael, CA: Presidio Press, 1978.

Moscow, Henry, *The Street Book.* New York: Hagstrom Company, Inc., 1978.

Myrick, David F., *San Francisco's Telegraph Hill.* Berkeley, CA: HowellNorth Books, 1972.

Reps, John W., *Cities of the American West.* Princeton, N.J.: Princeton University Press.

Rowland, Leon, *Los Fundadores.* Fresno: Academy of California Church History, 1951.

Soule, Frank; Gihon, John; and Nisbett, James, *The Annals of San Francisco.* Palo Alto, CA: Lewis Osborne, 1966.

Reports and Other Documents

Adams, Elizabeth G. *Street Names in San Francisco.* An unpublished paper, 1954.

A Guide to Historic San Francisco. San Francisco History Room, San Francisco Public Library, 1980.

Colorful Place Names of Northern California. Wells Fargo Bank, San Francisco: 1974.

Municipal Record of San Francisco, 1882 and 1909.

Murphy, Edward. *The Thoroughfares of San Francisco.* An unpublished and undated paper.

Official Journal of the Proceedings of the Board of Supervisors, Volume IV, November, 1909.

Raphael, Brother L. *A Guide to the History of St. Mary's College Campus.* 1983 and 1990.

San Francisco Directory, 1861.

Magazine Articles

Brown, Thomas P., "San Francisco's CenturyOld Street NamesThe Happy Valley Days of '49," *The Time Card,* San Francisco: The Transportation Club of San Francisco, 1949.

Maupin, Armistead. "The Streets of San Francisco," *New West,* Los Angeles: May 23, 1977.

San Jose Pioneer Magazine, September 15, 1897.

Wheelan, Albert P. "The Streets, Avenues, Alleys and Lanes of South of Market—The Story of Their Origin," *South of Market Journal,* San Francisco: April, 1927.

Newspapers

Fitzhammon, E.G. "The Streets of San Francisco," *San Francisco Chronicle,* August 27, 1928–March 31, 1929.

San Francisco Chronicle, various issues.

San Francisco Examiner, various issues.

Tukman, John. "Naming History," *Mt. Tamalpais Blazer,* January 24, 1985.

New York Times, June 9, 1988

Richmond Review, June 1990